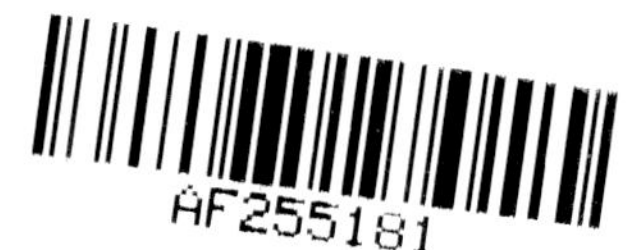

Outside the Box

Stack Savage

To my three children, Zeke, Reu and Shi. Who continue to inspire me, my art, and the world around us.

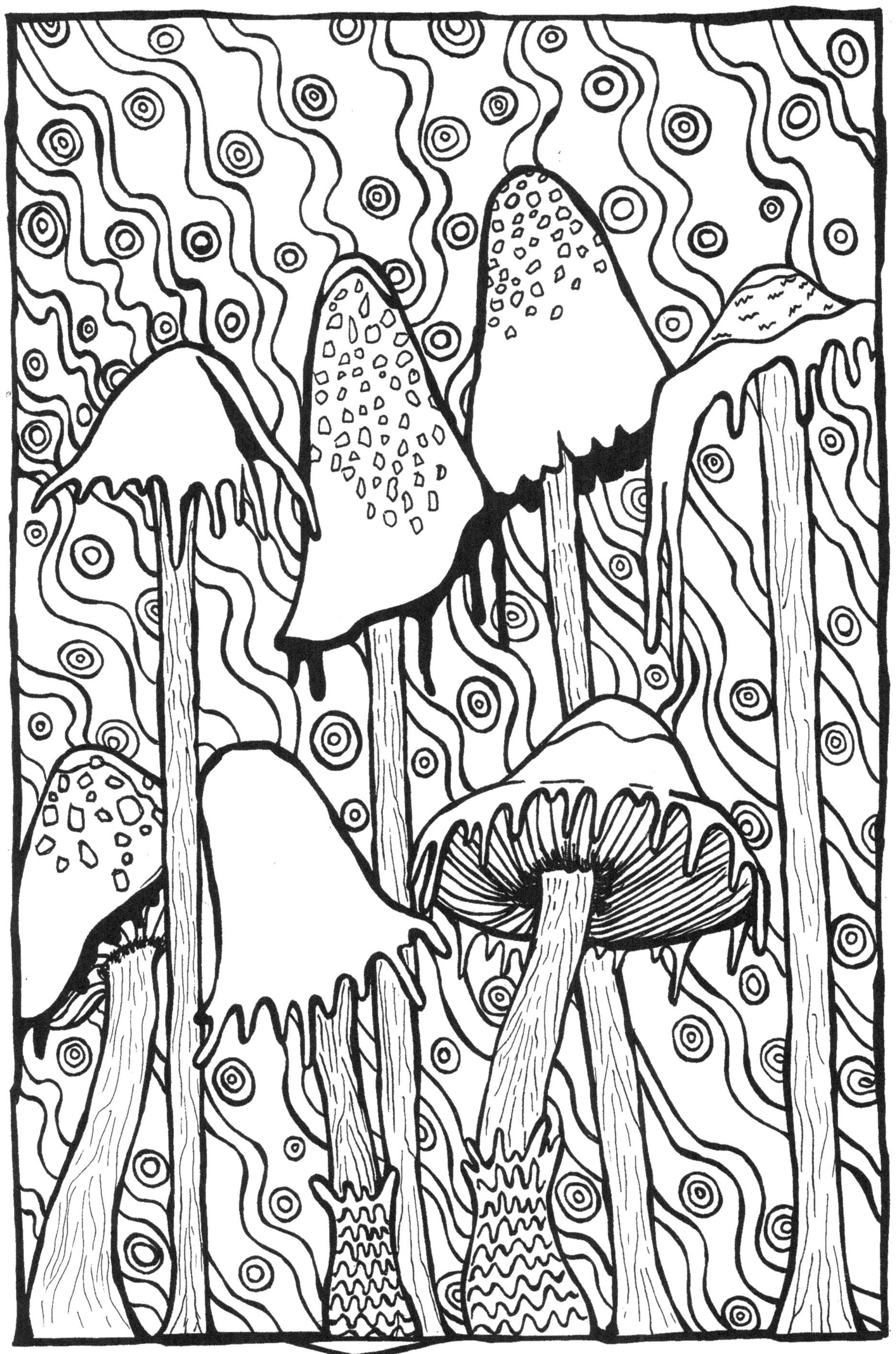

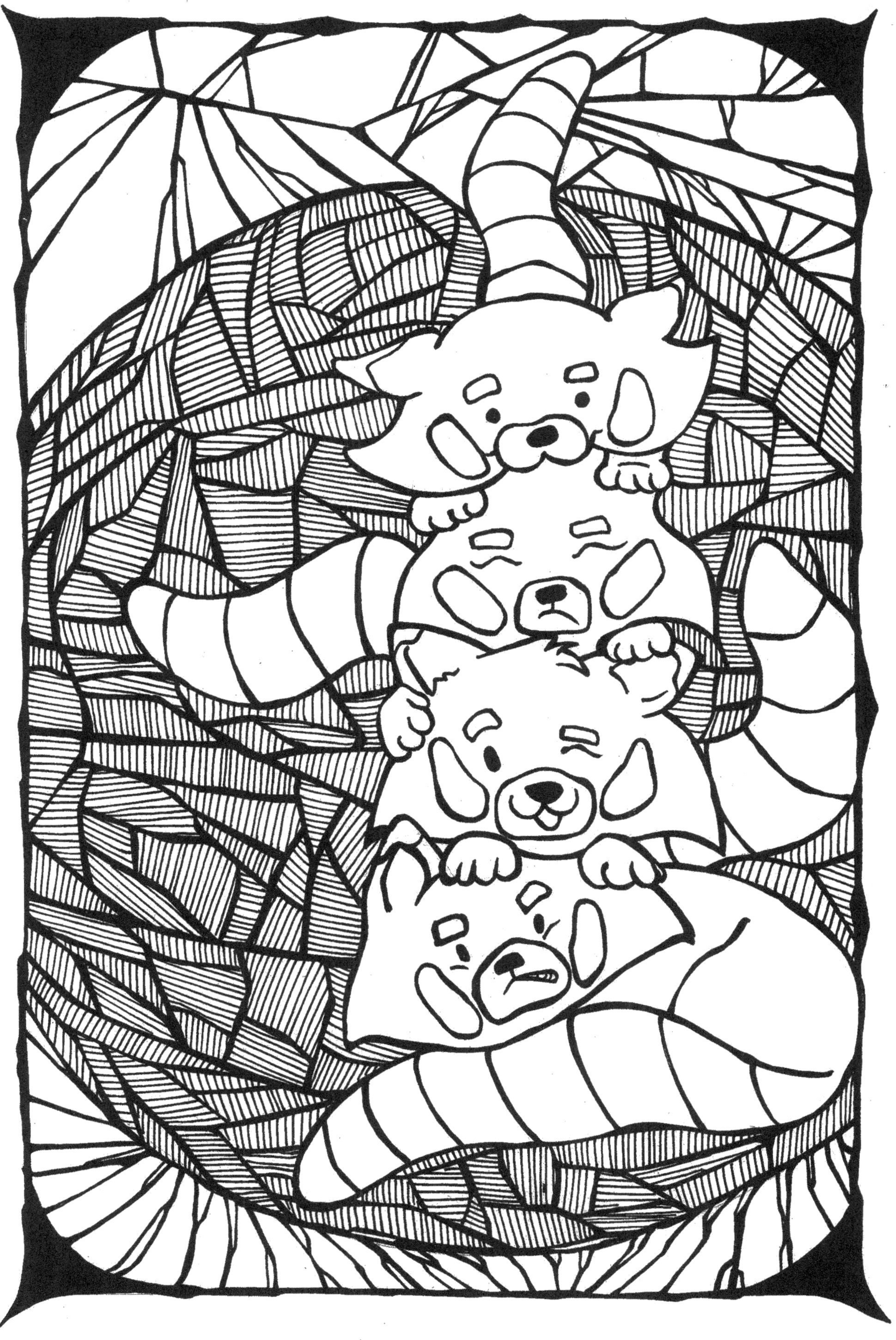

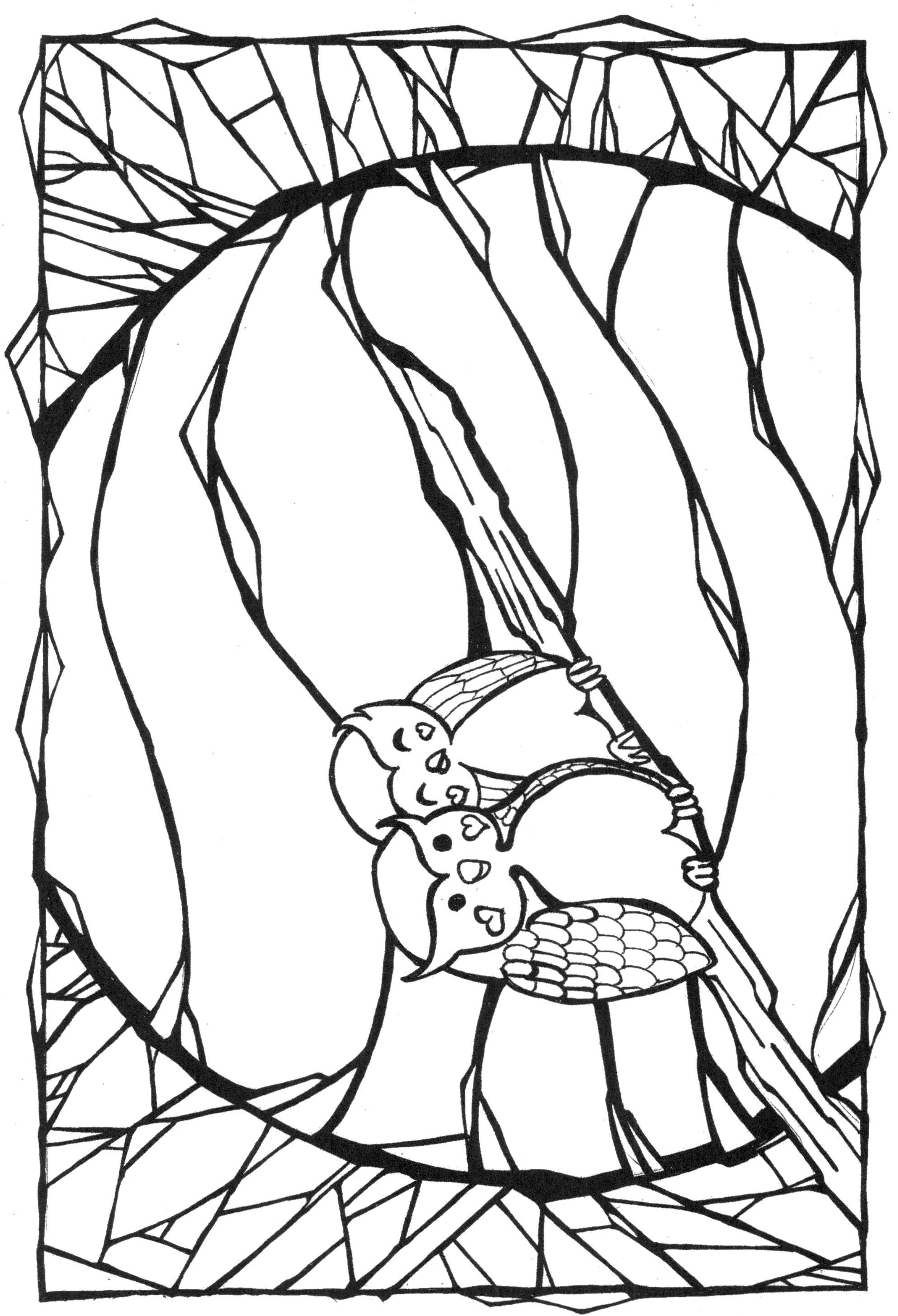

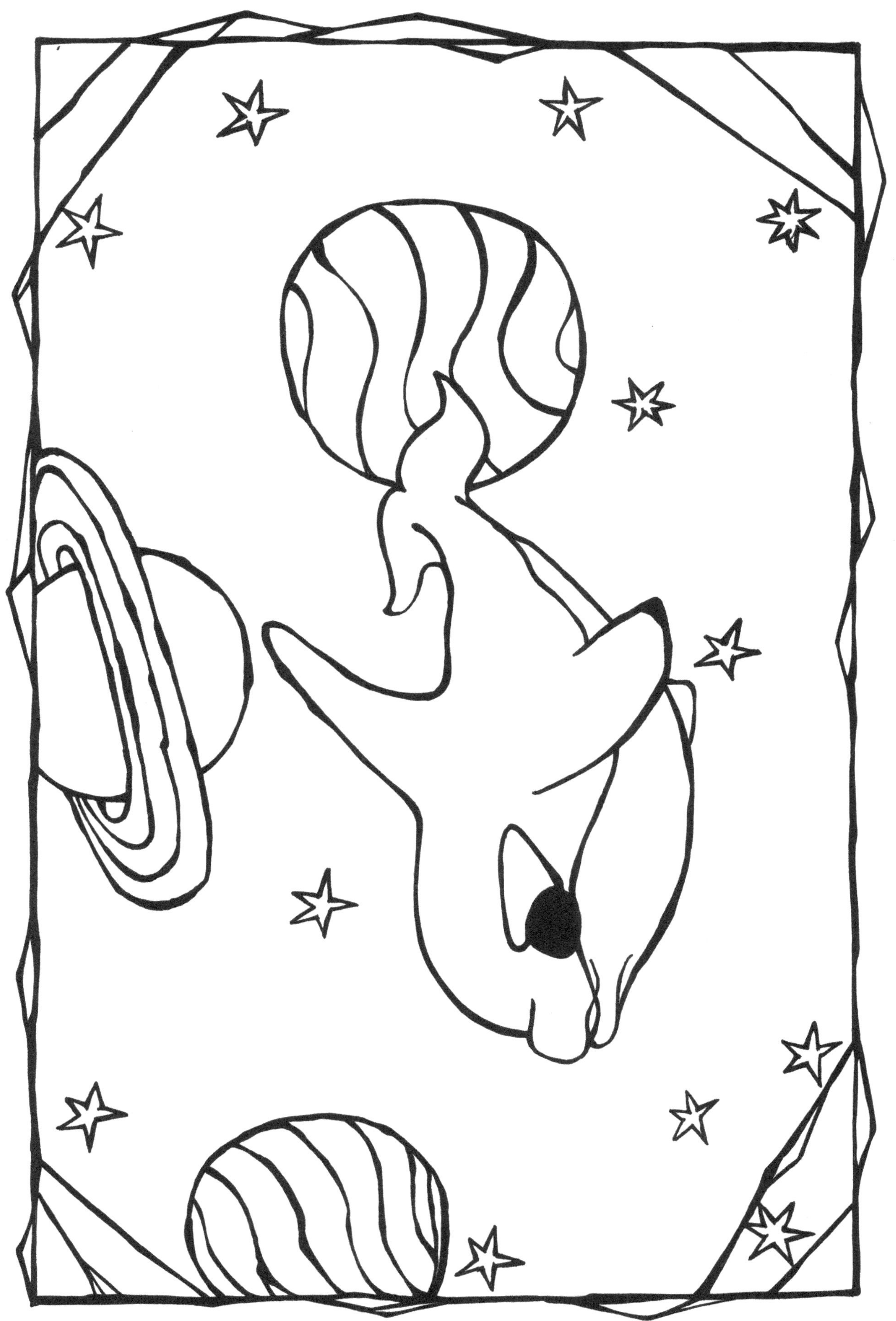

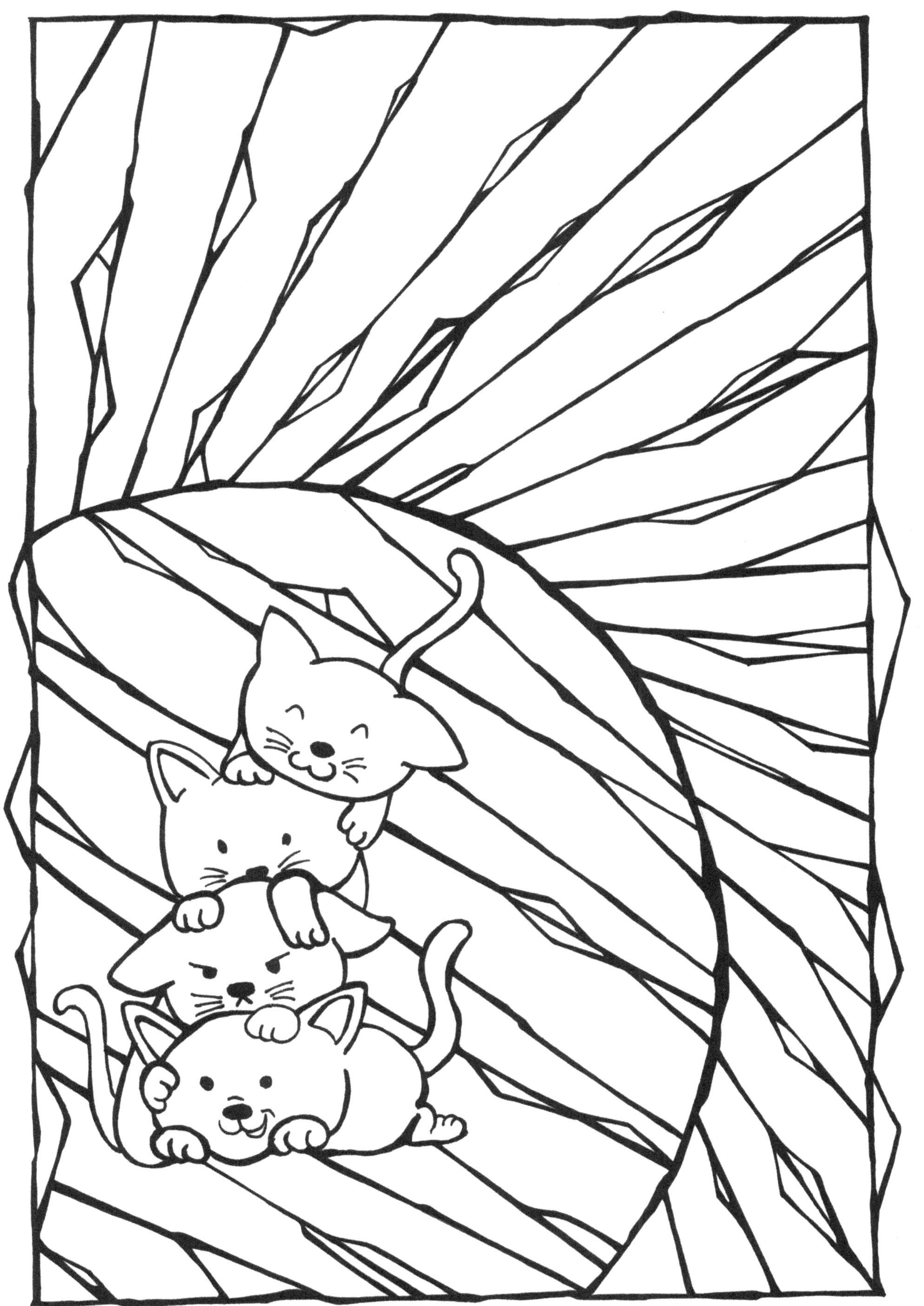

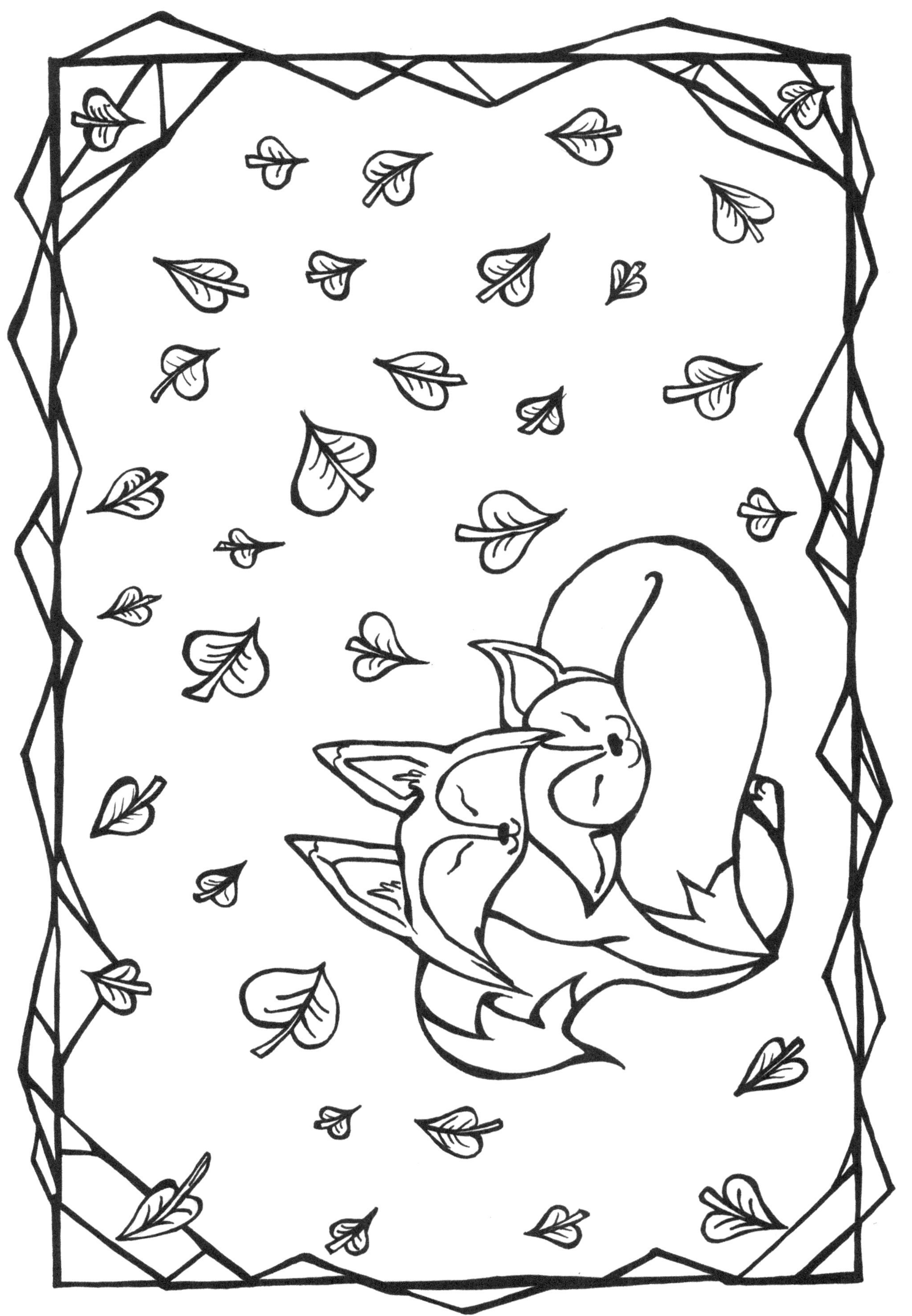

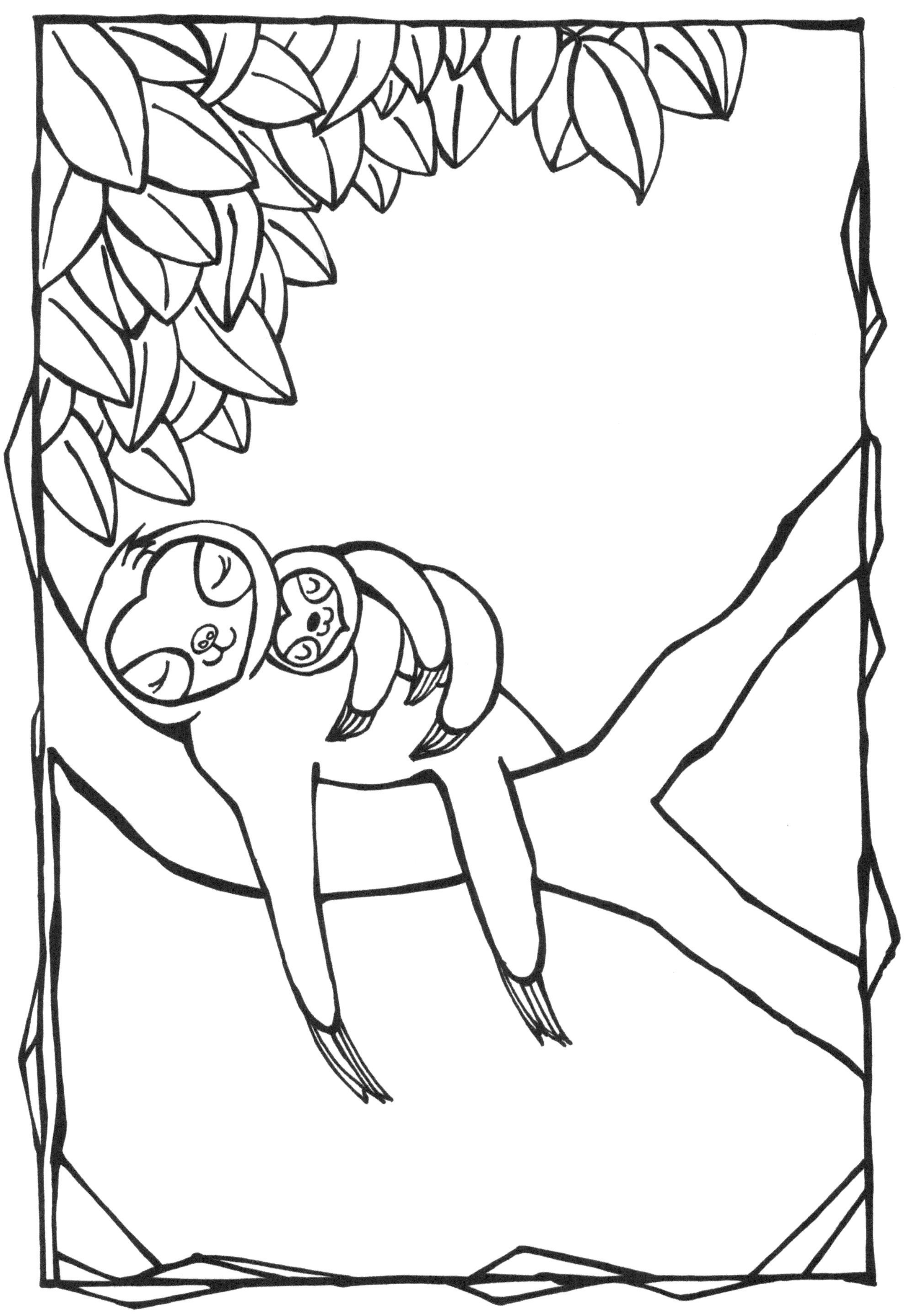

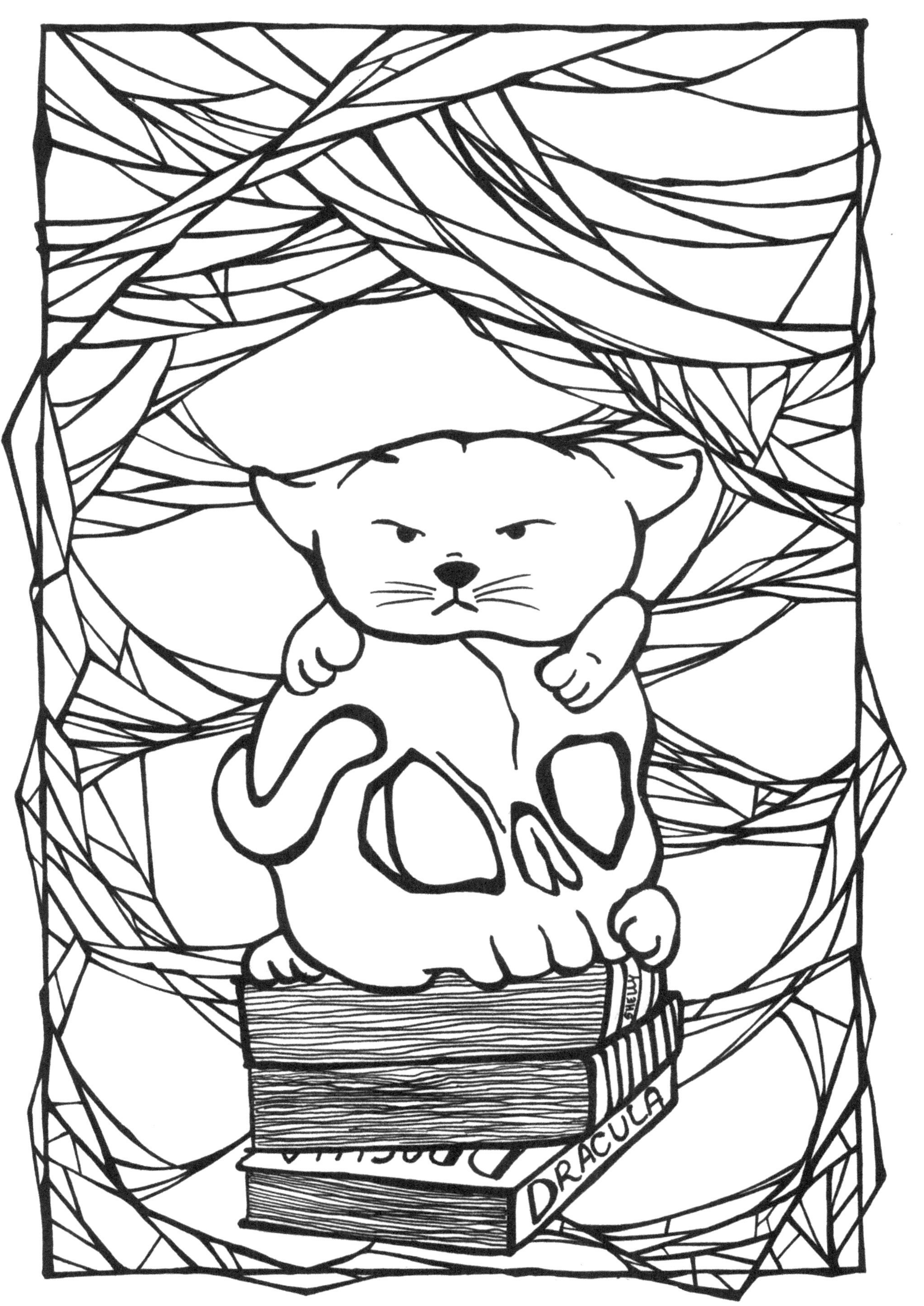

SHELLY
DRACULA
Dracula

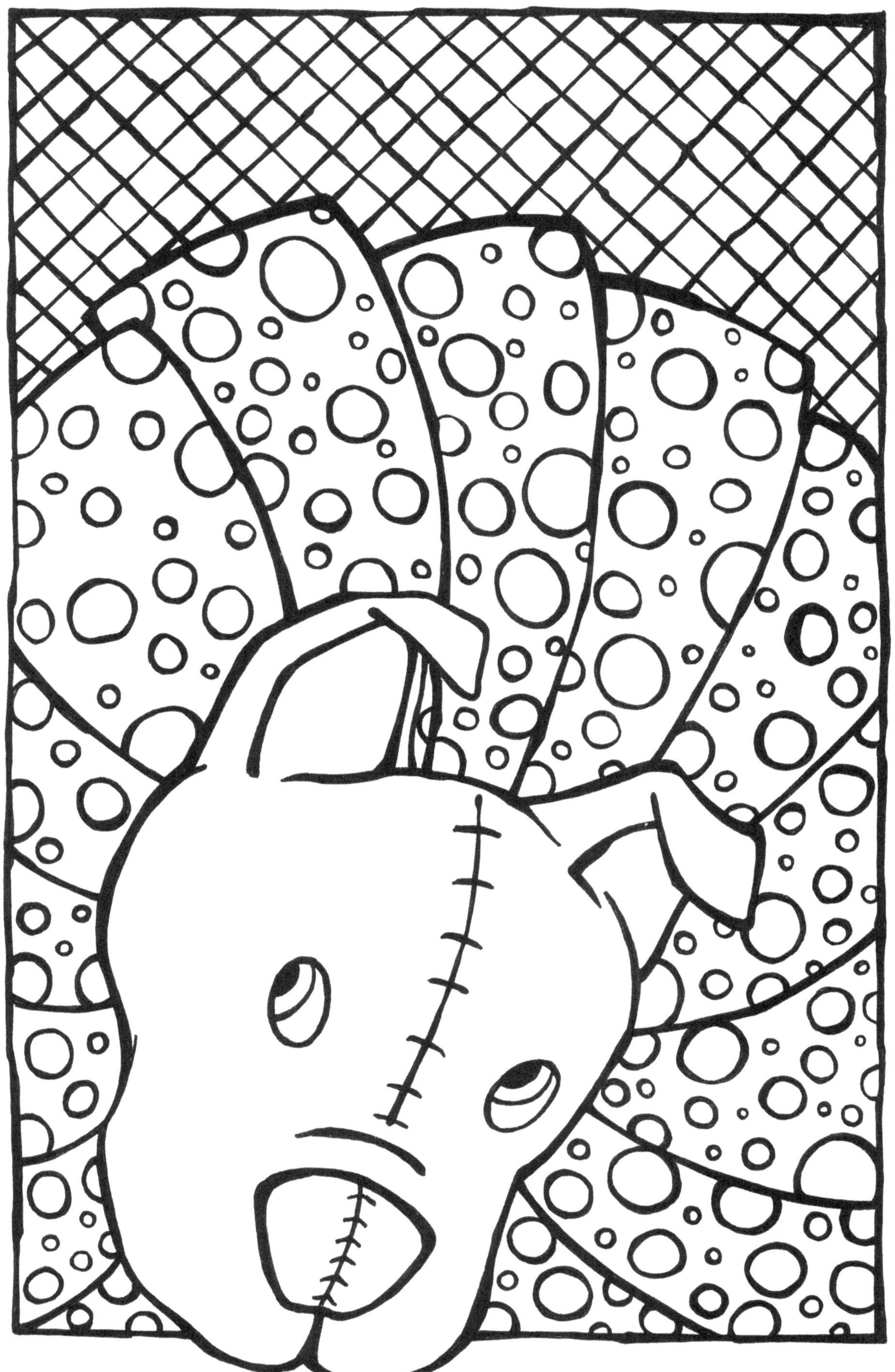

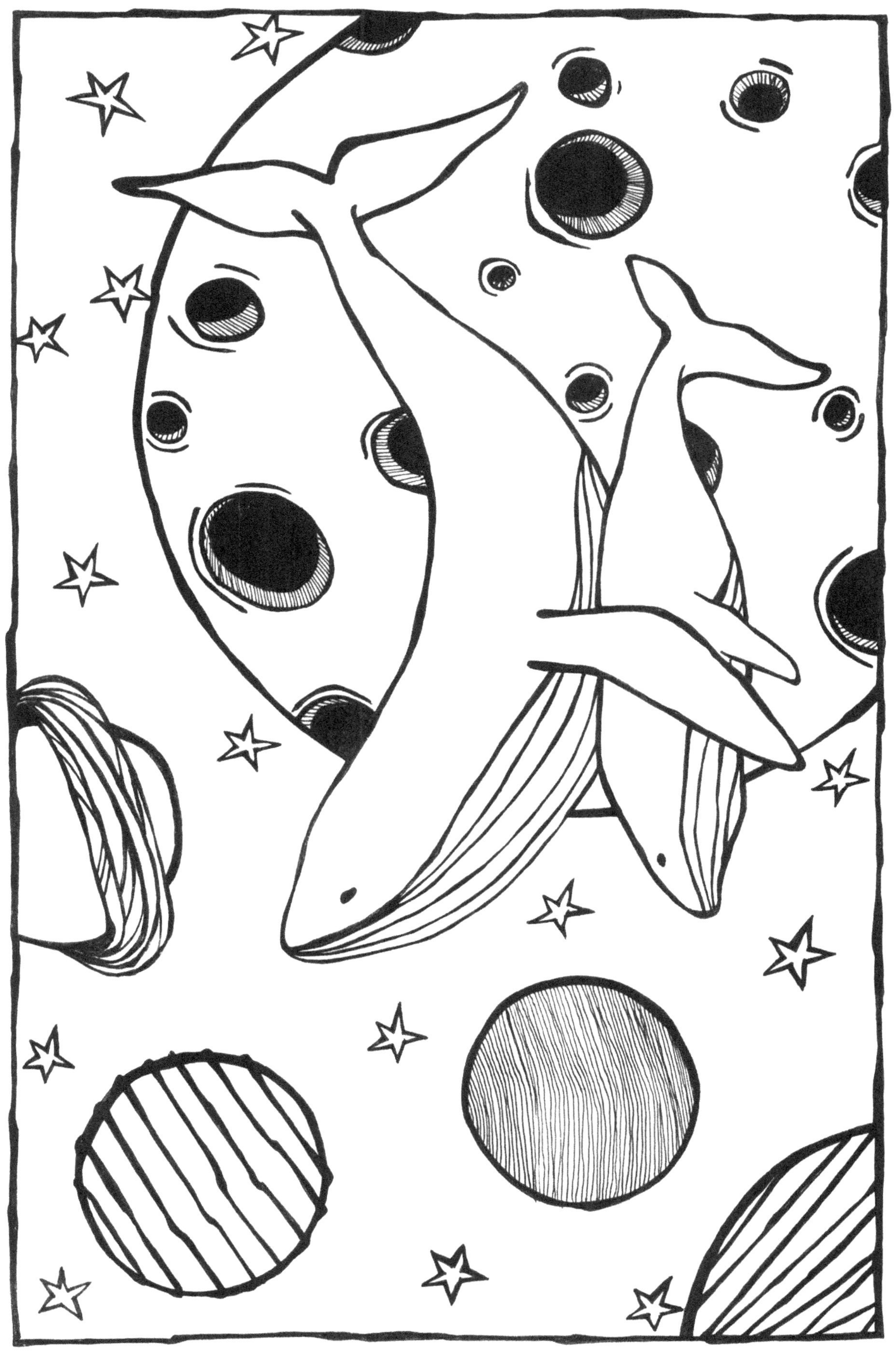

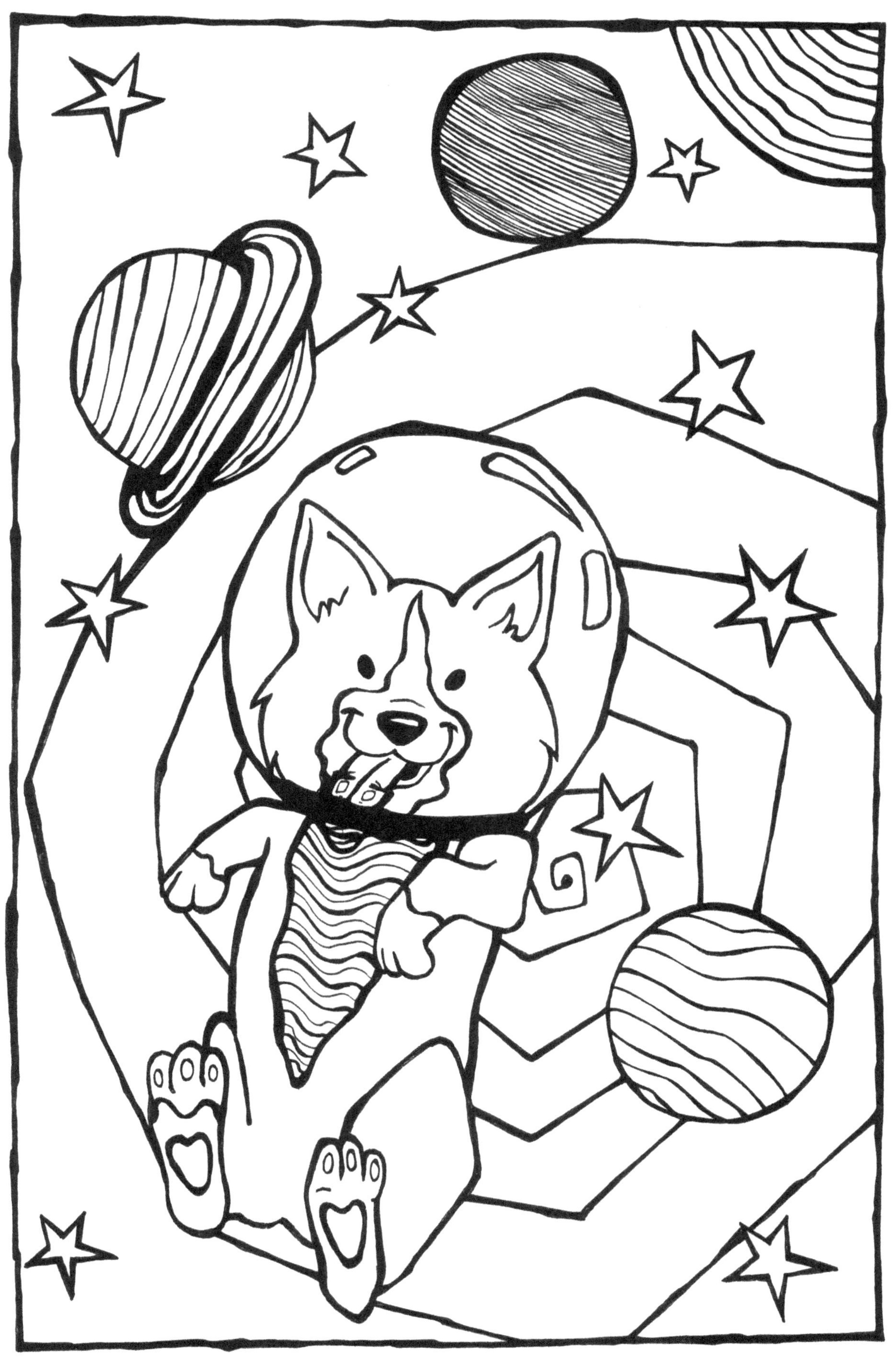

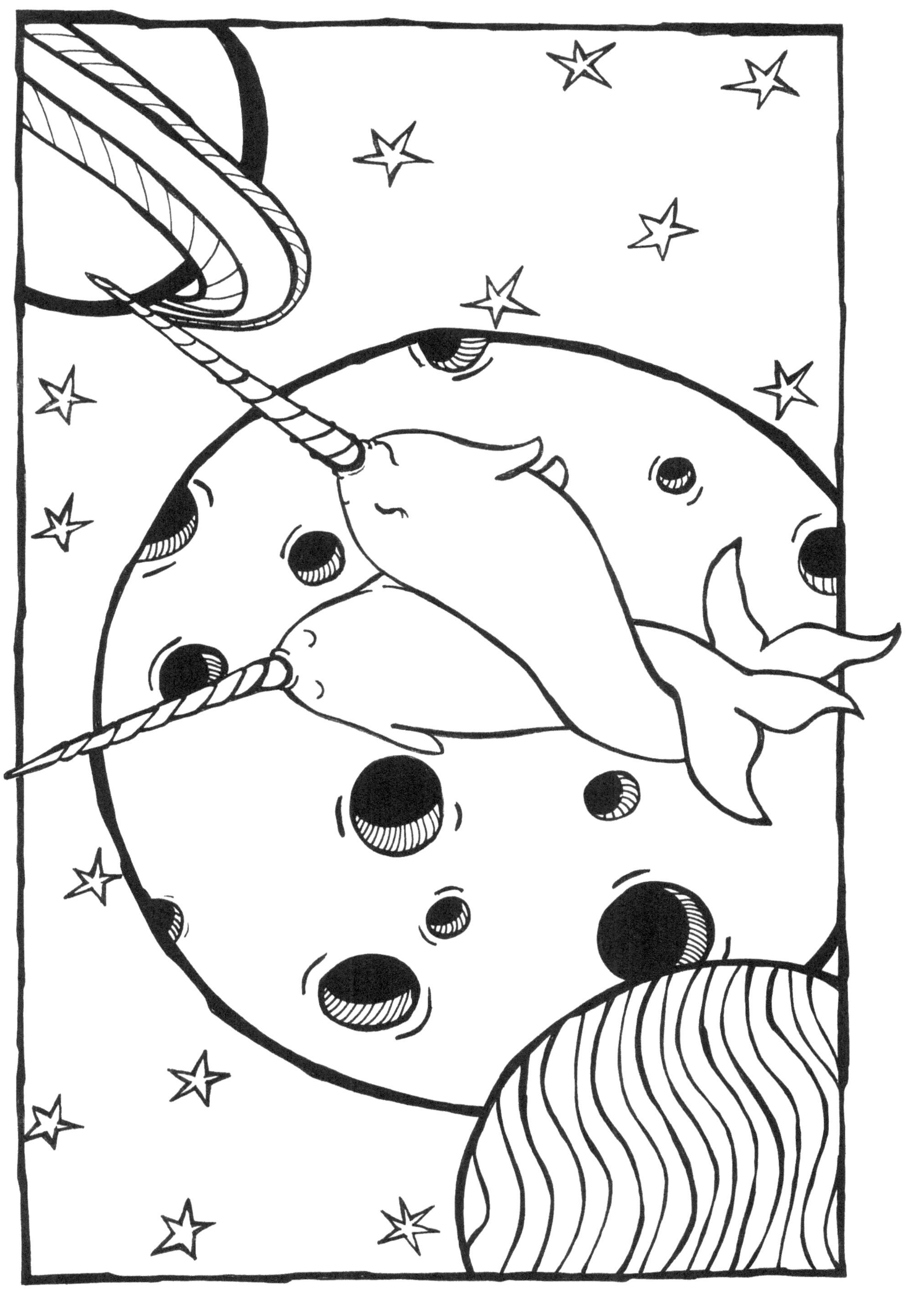

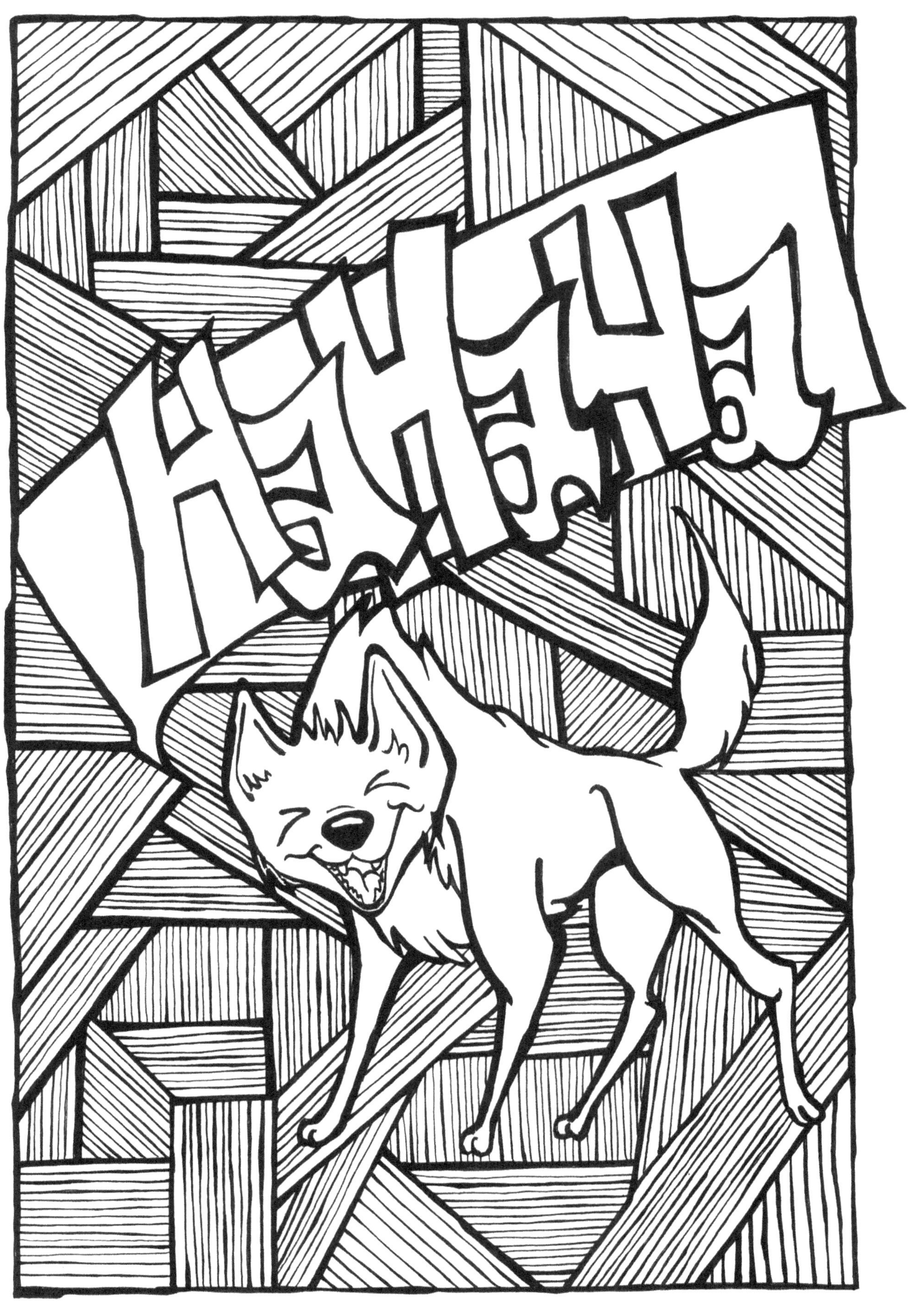
HaHaHaHa

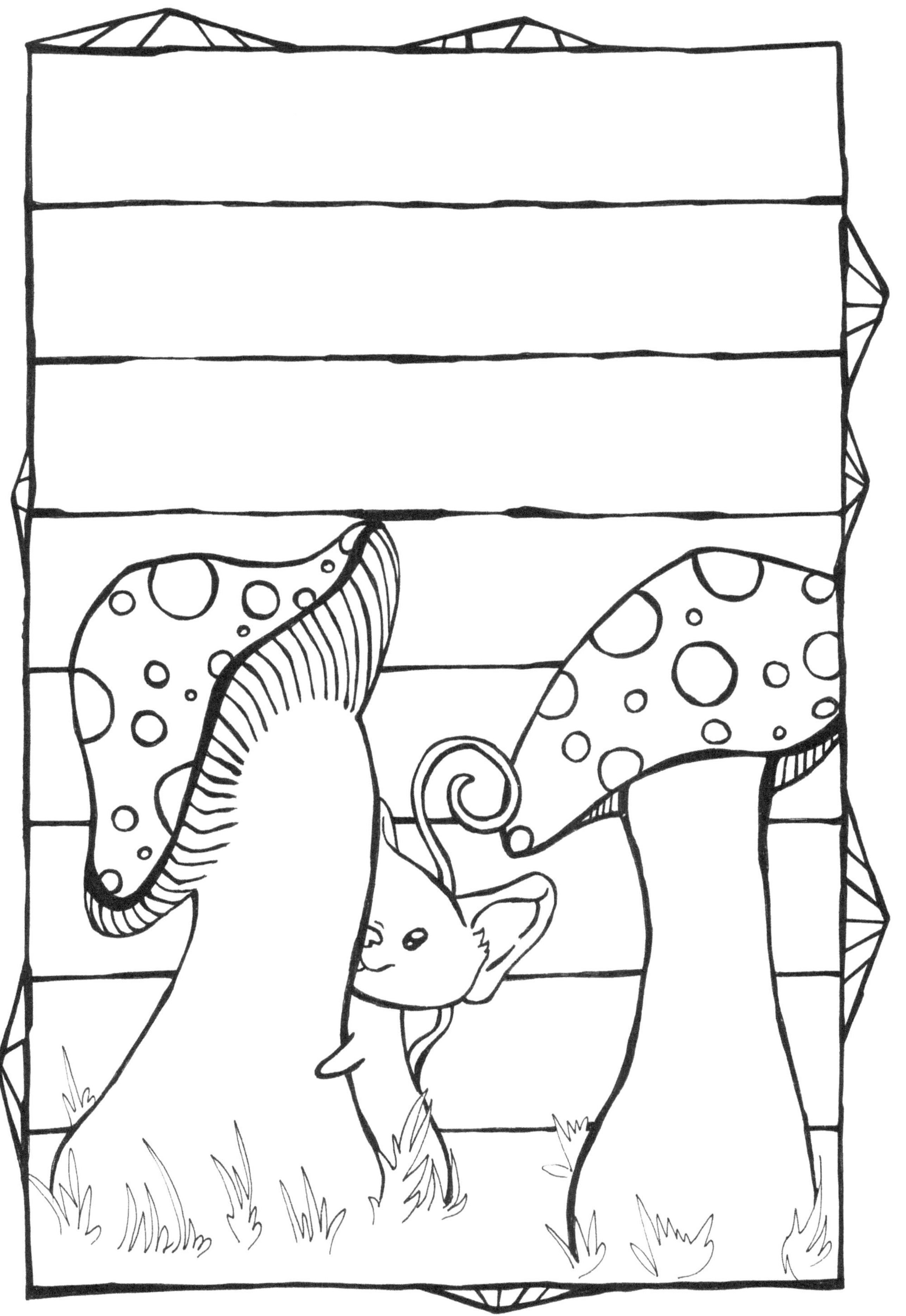

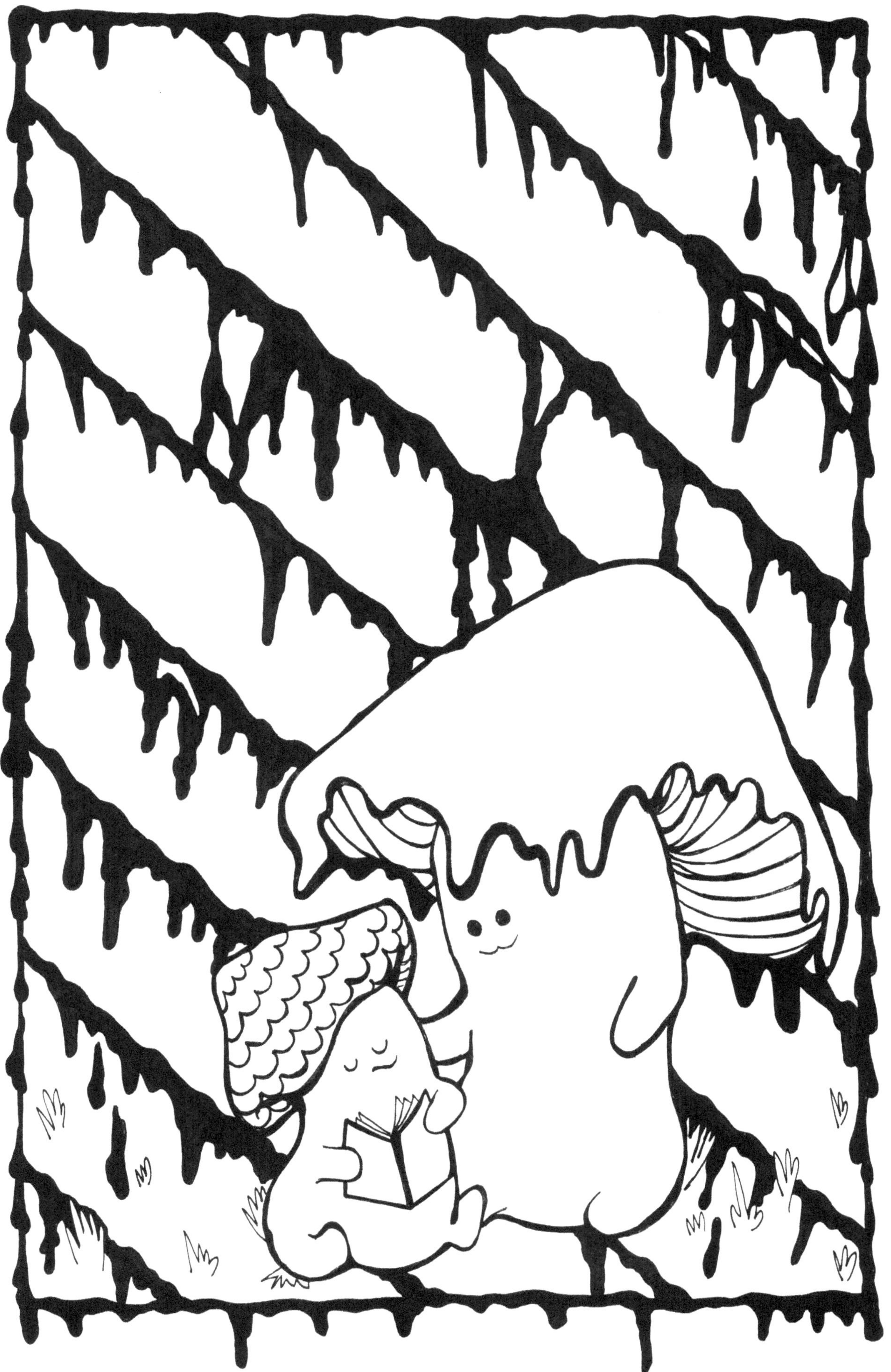

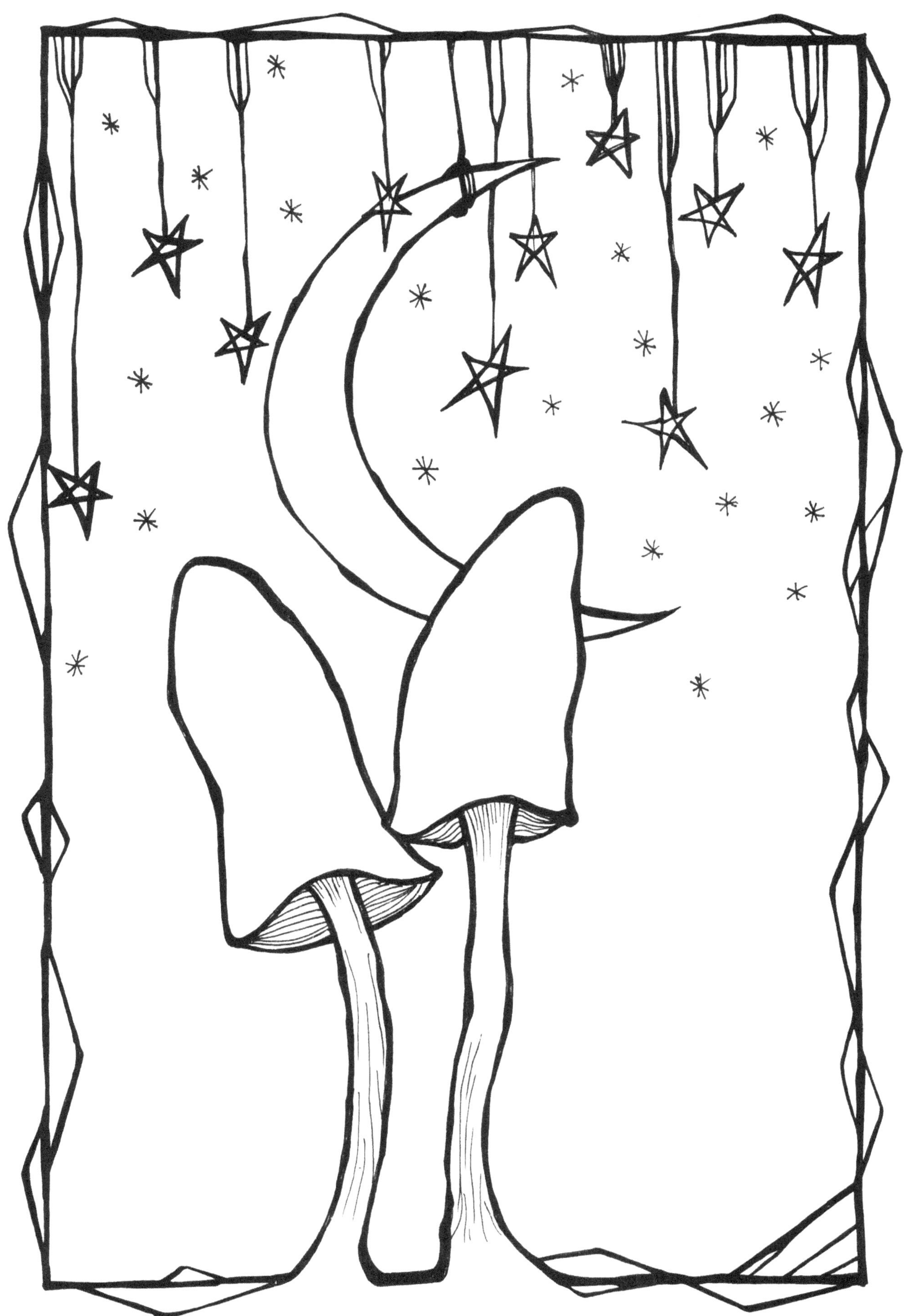

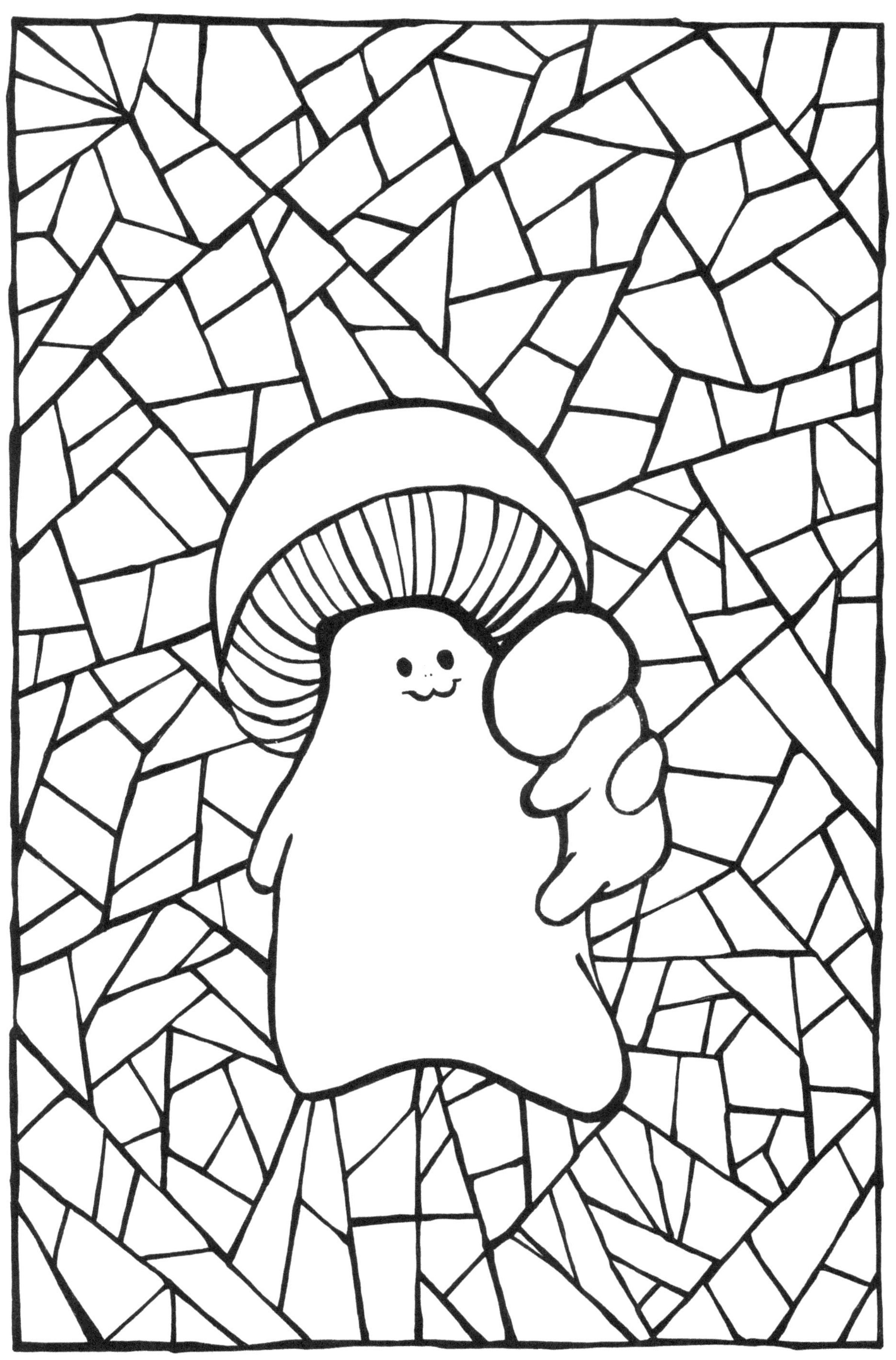

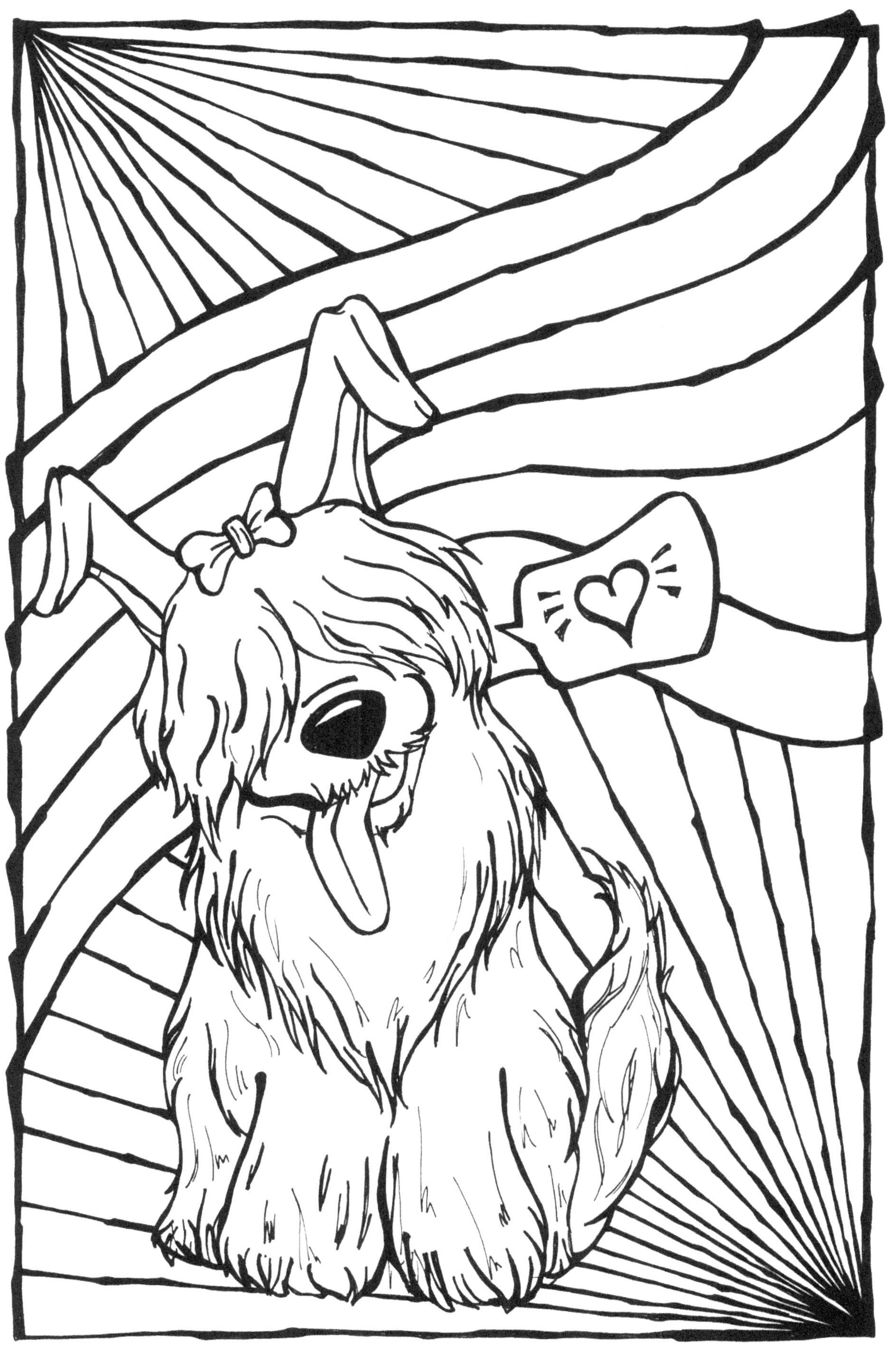

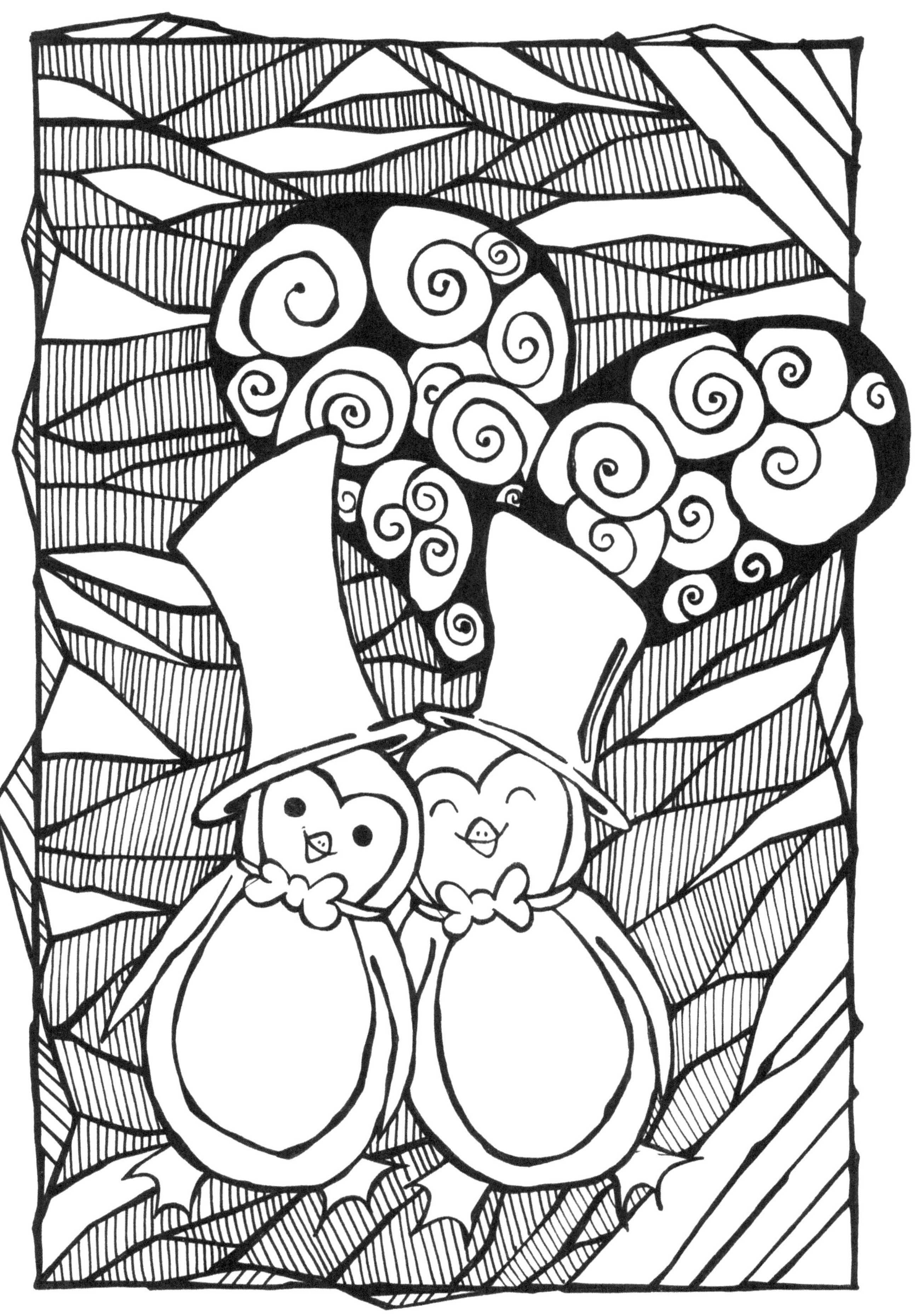

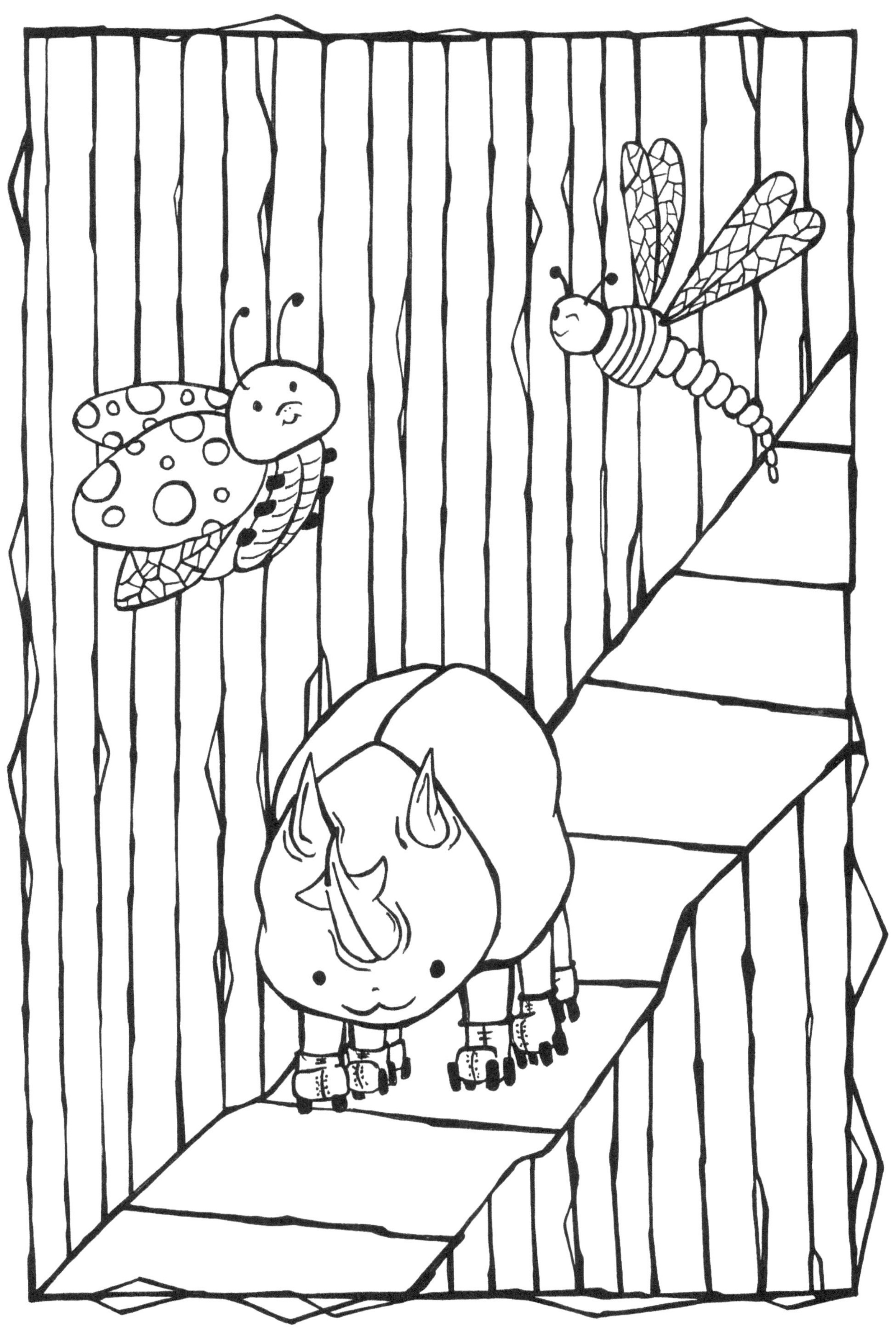

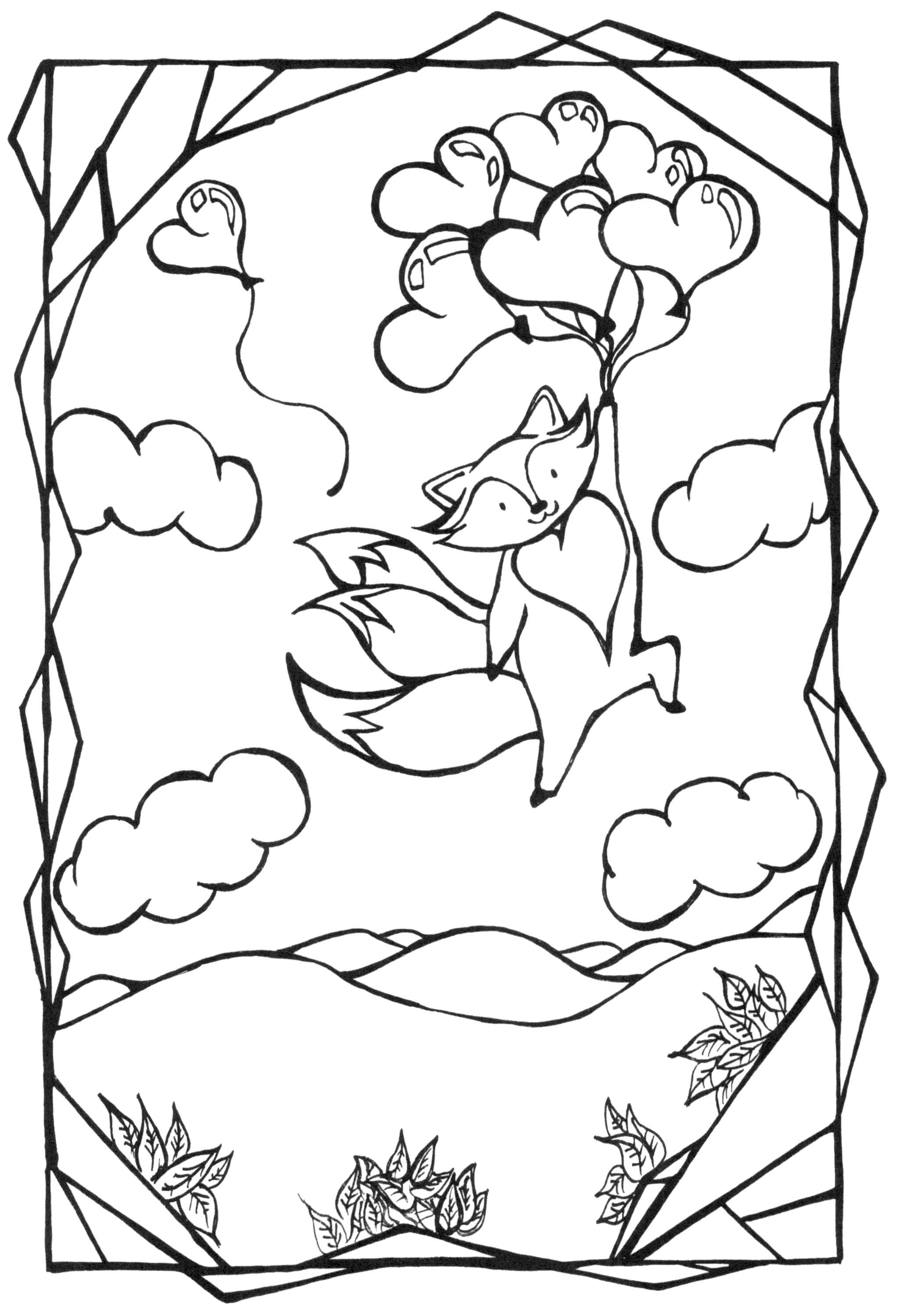

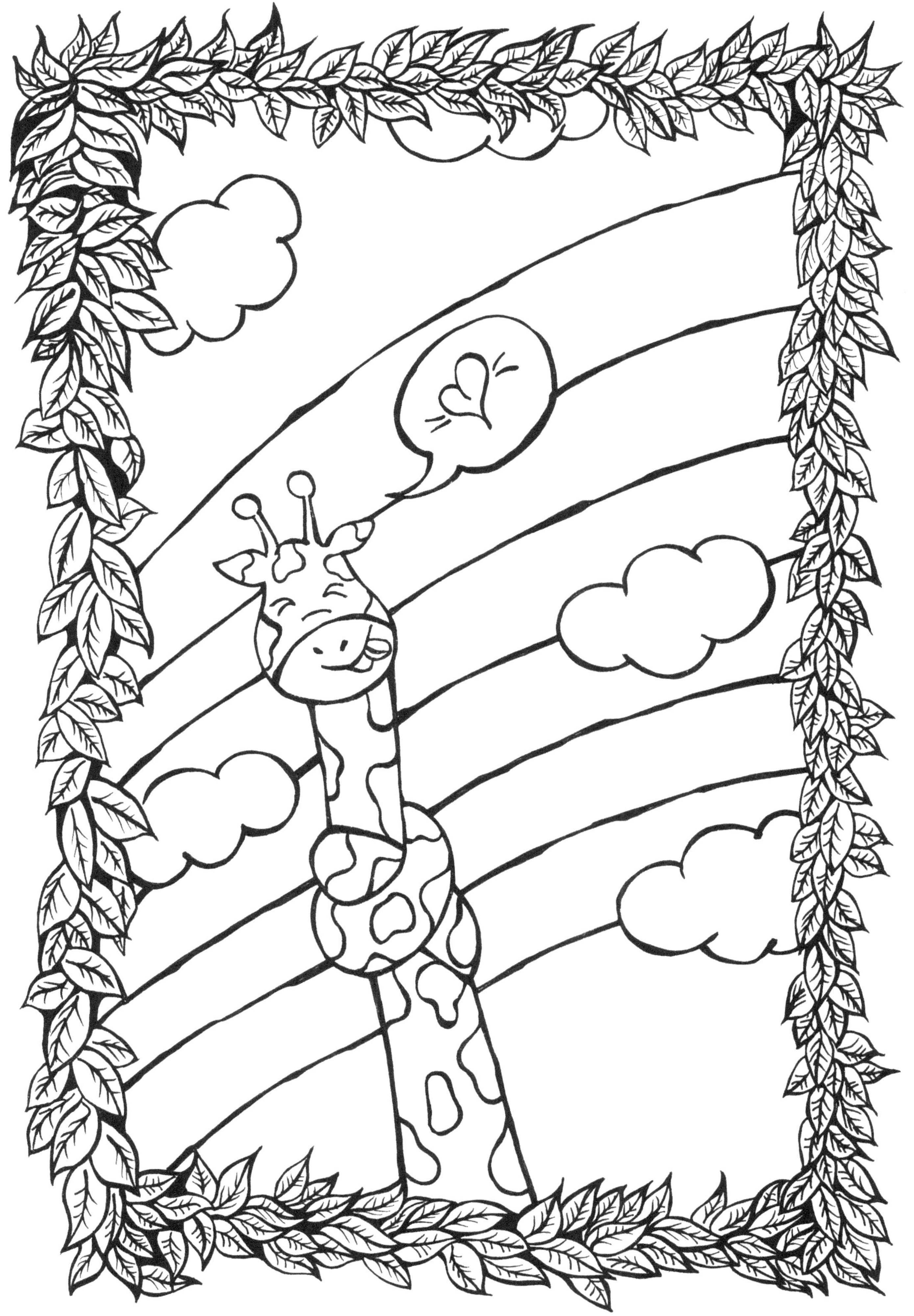

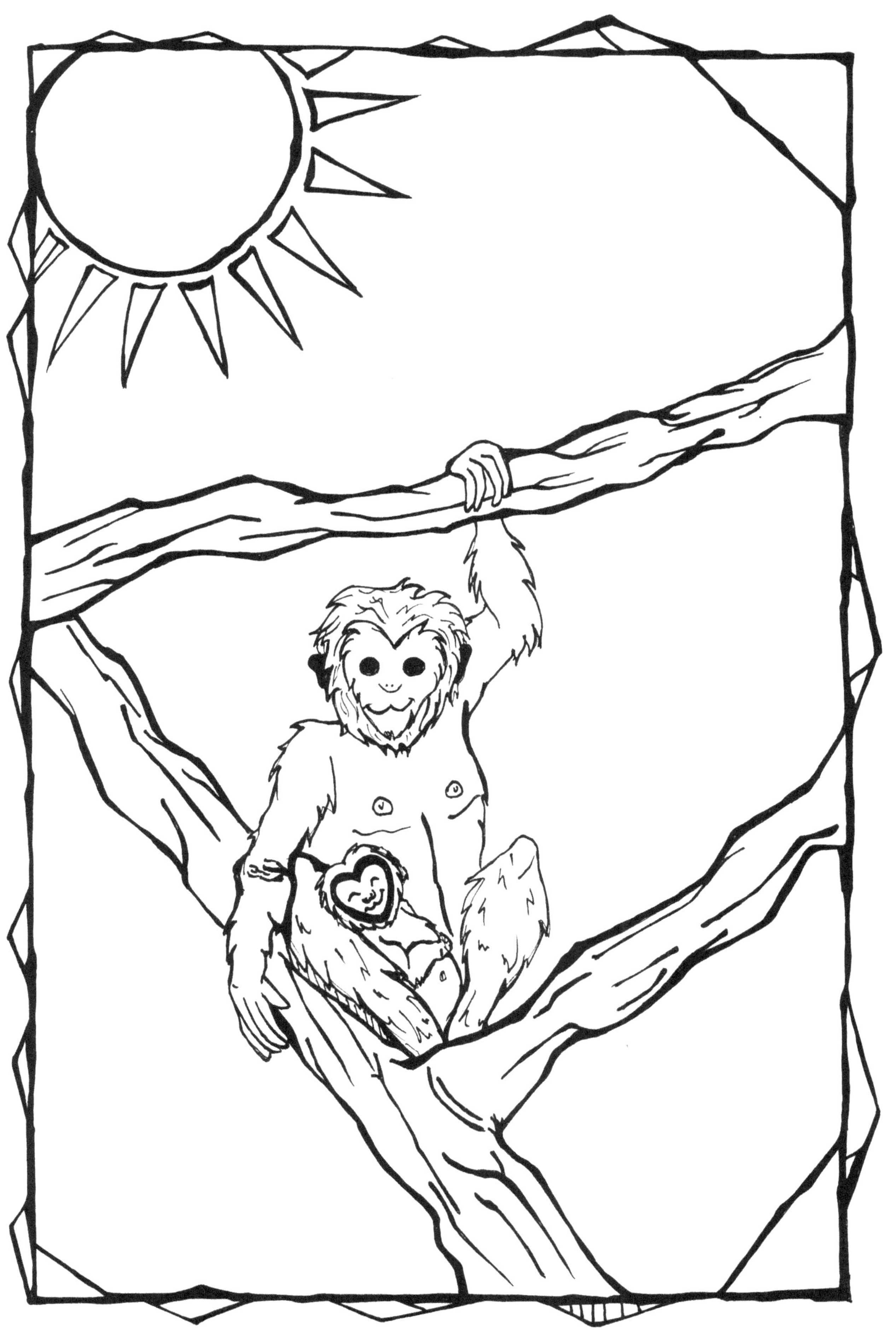

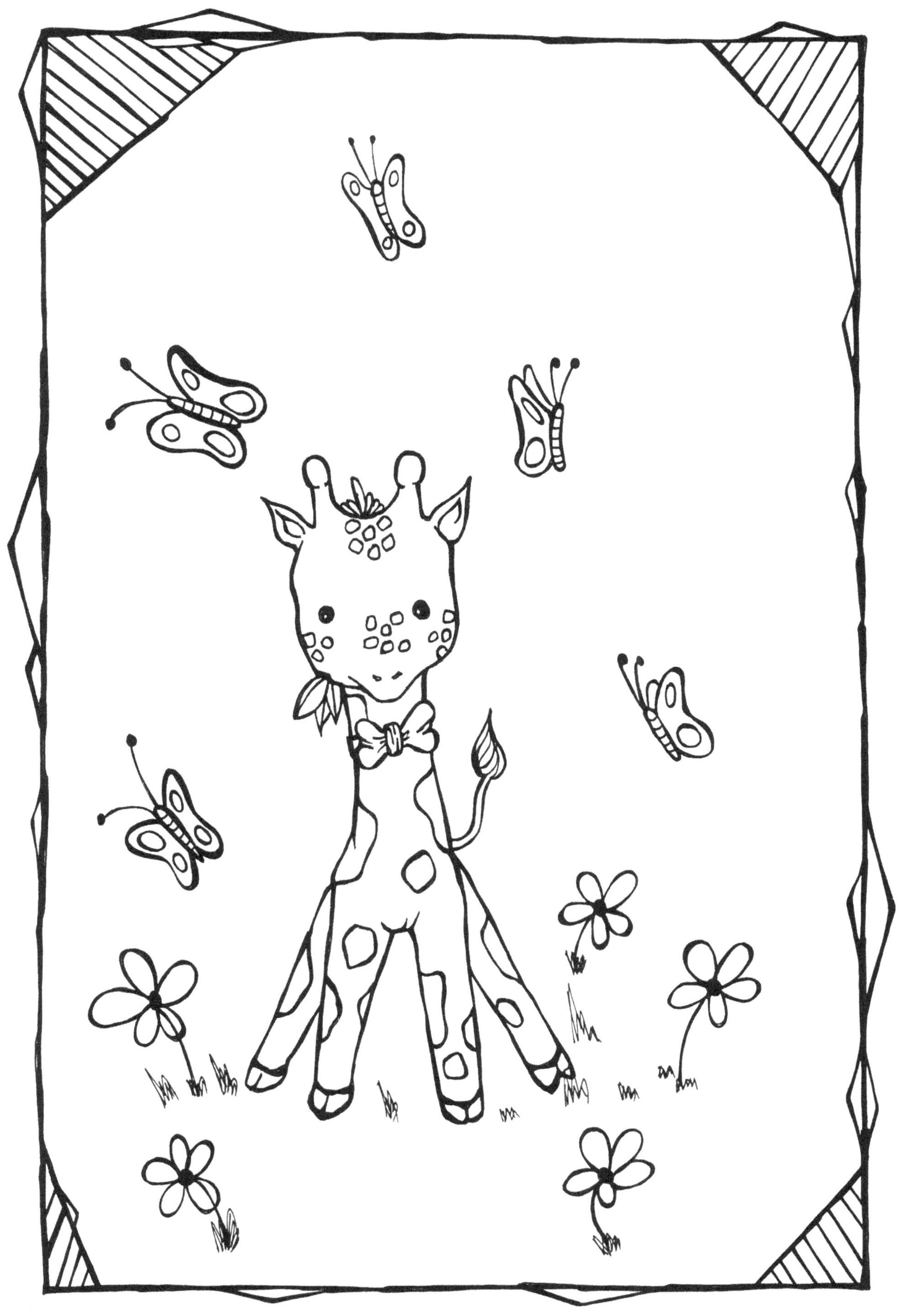

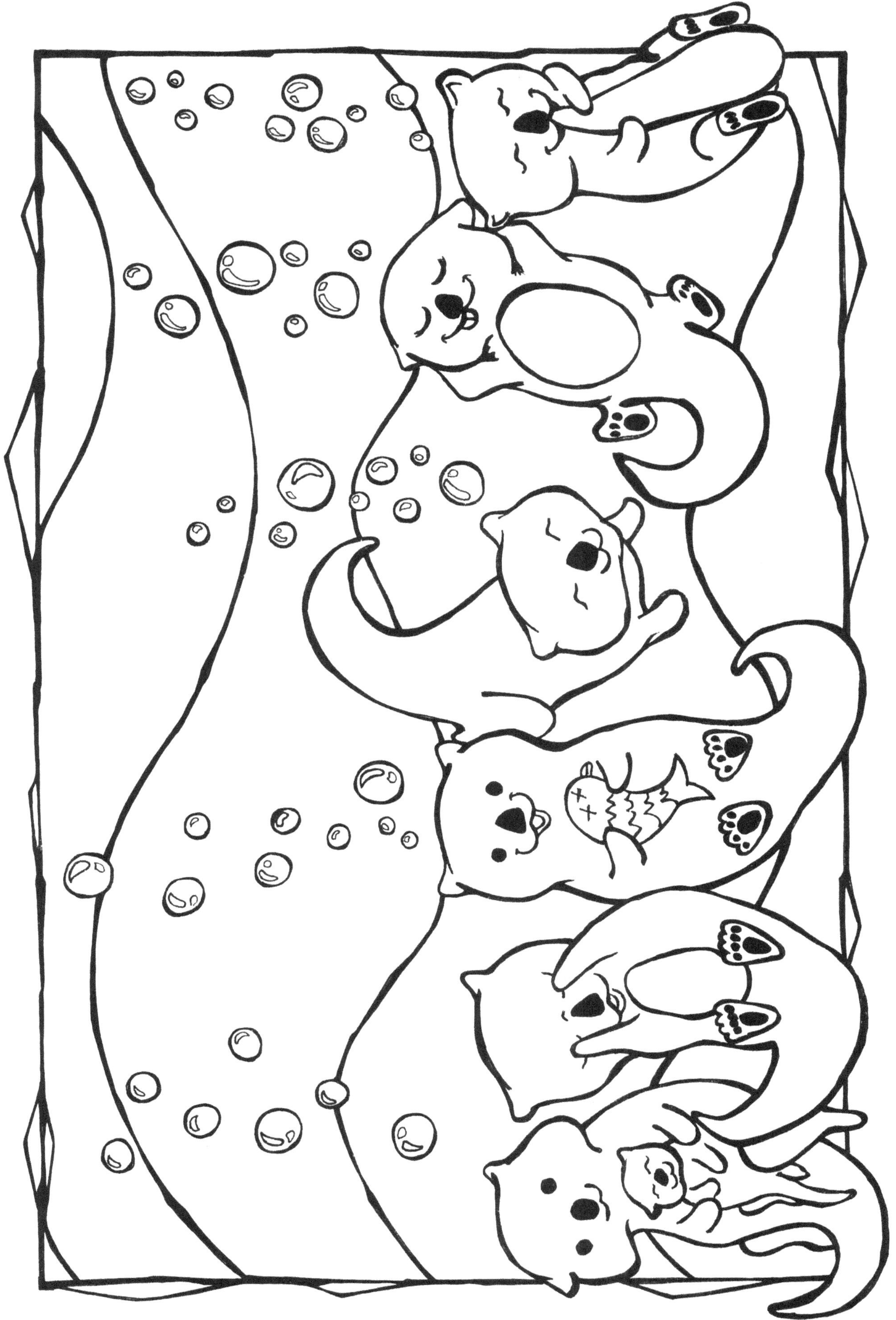

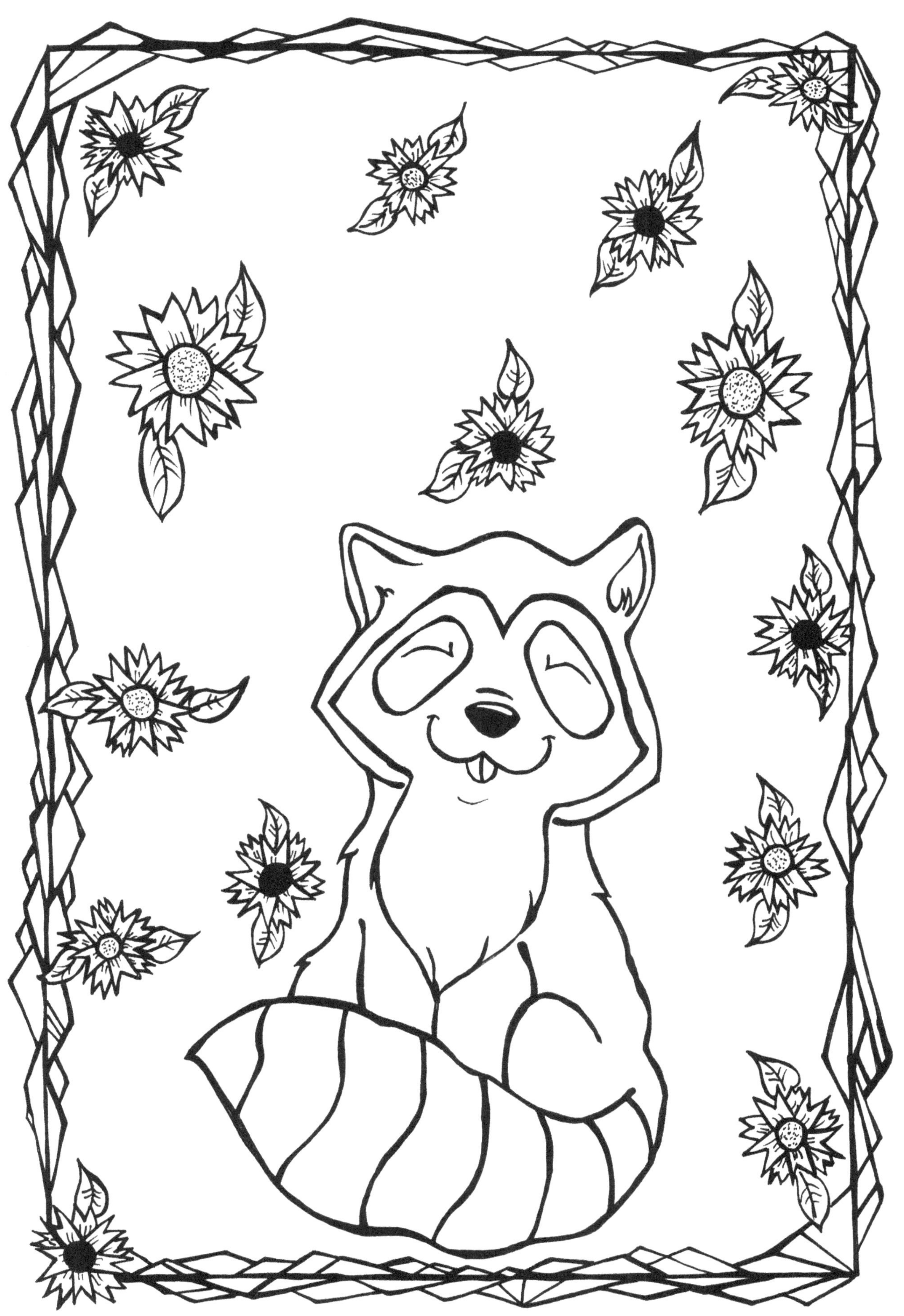

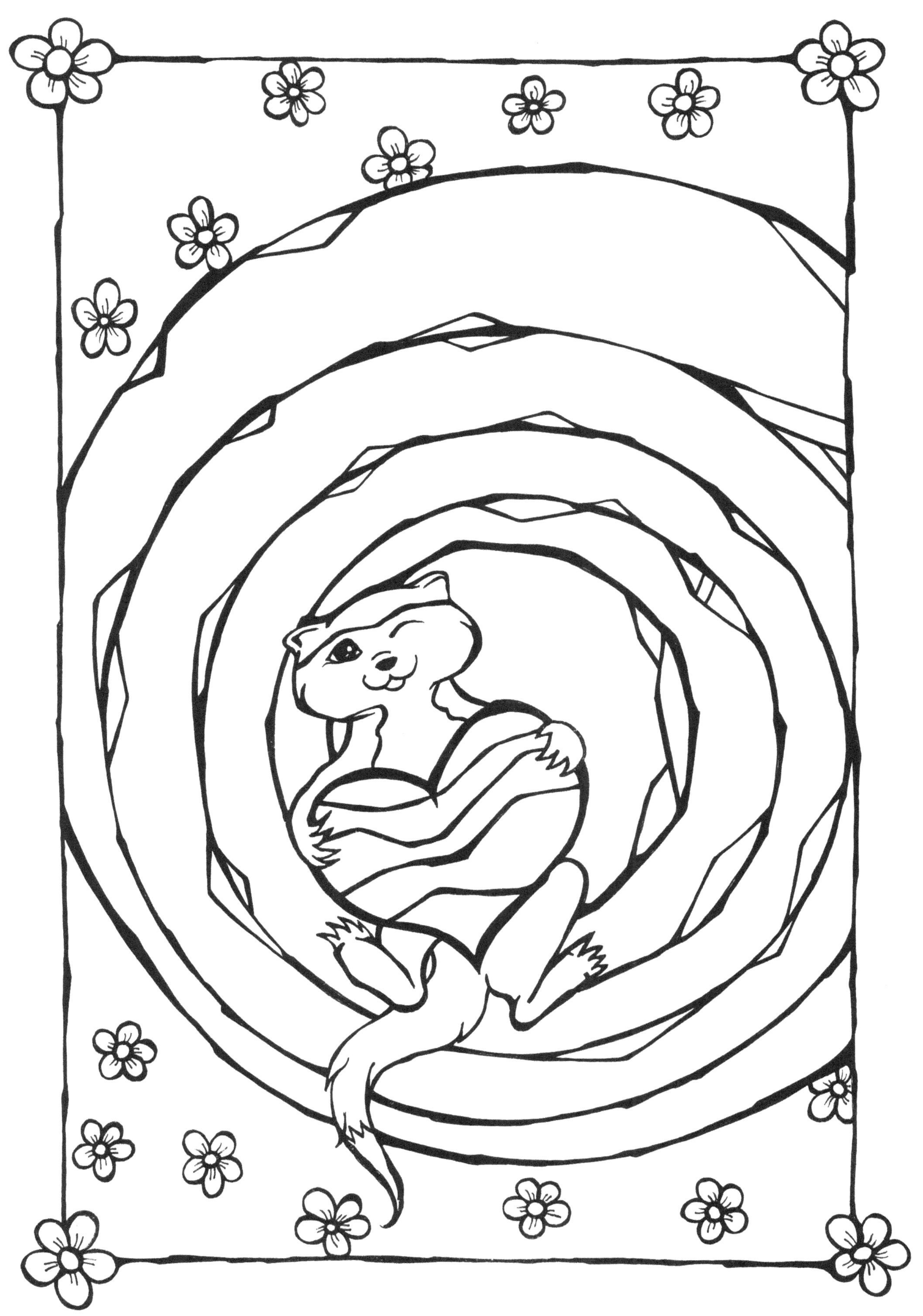

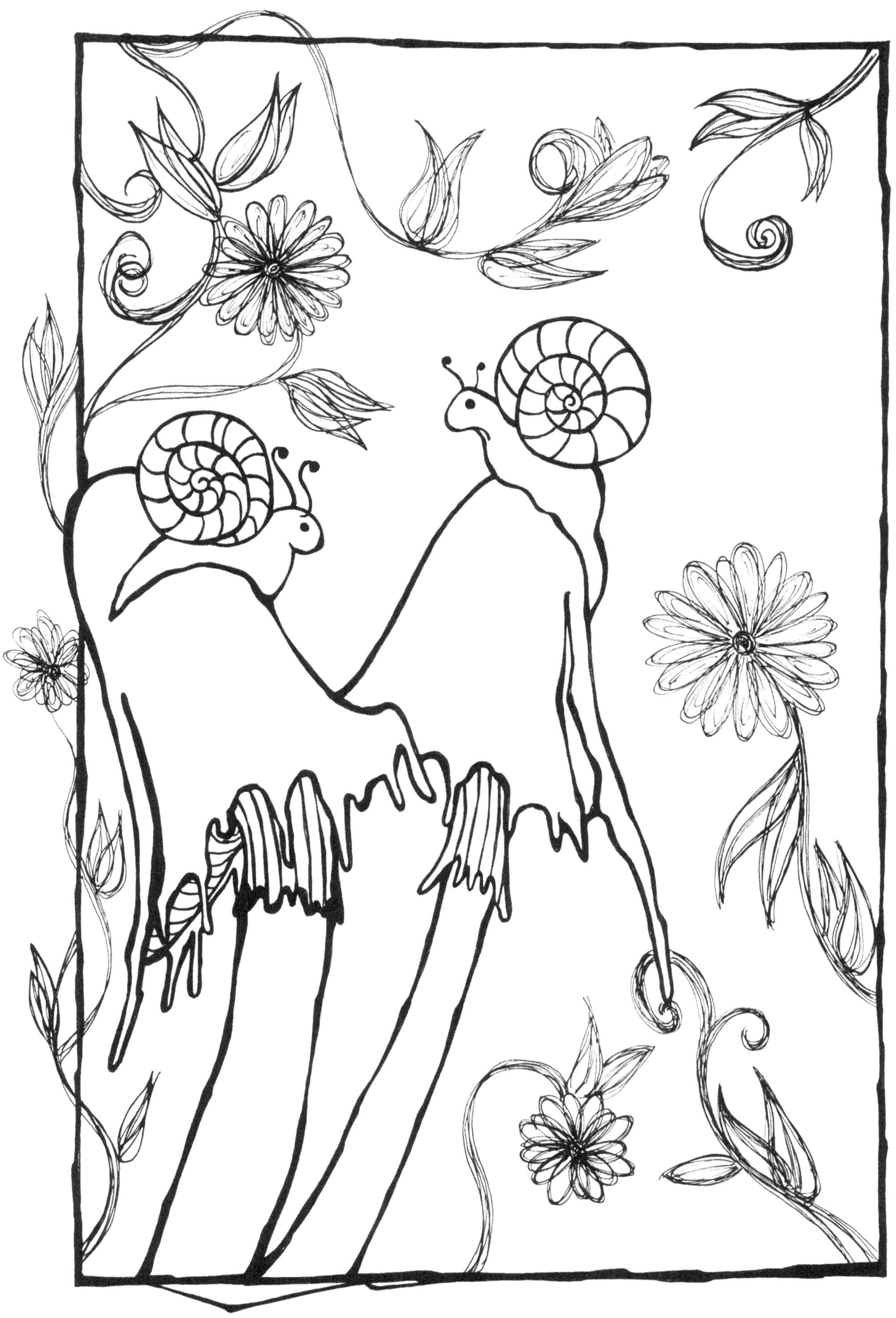

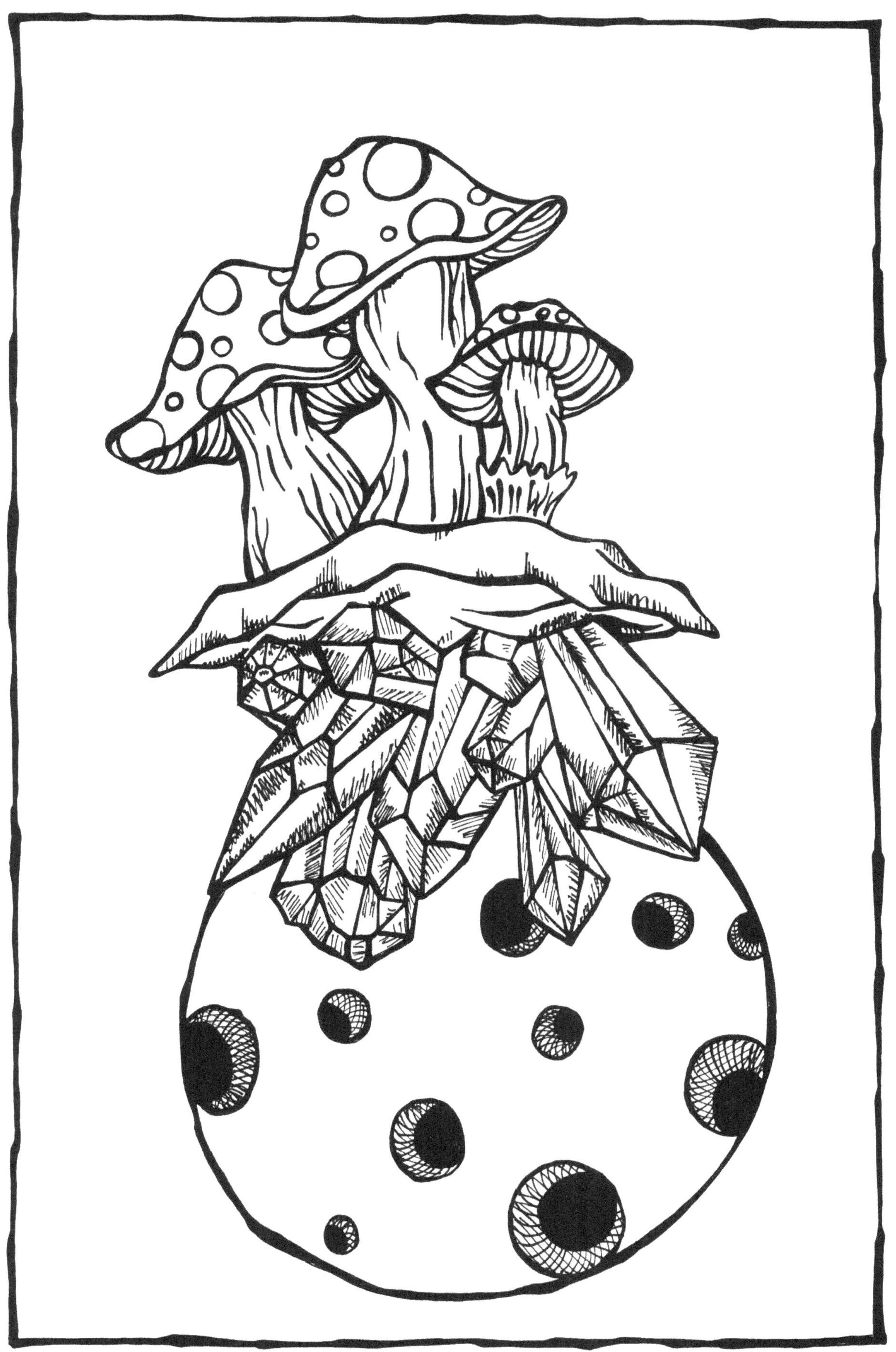

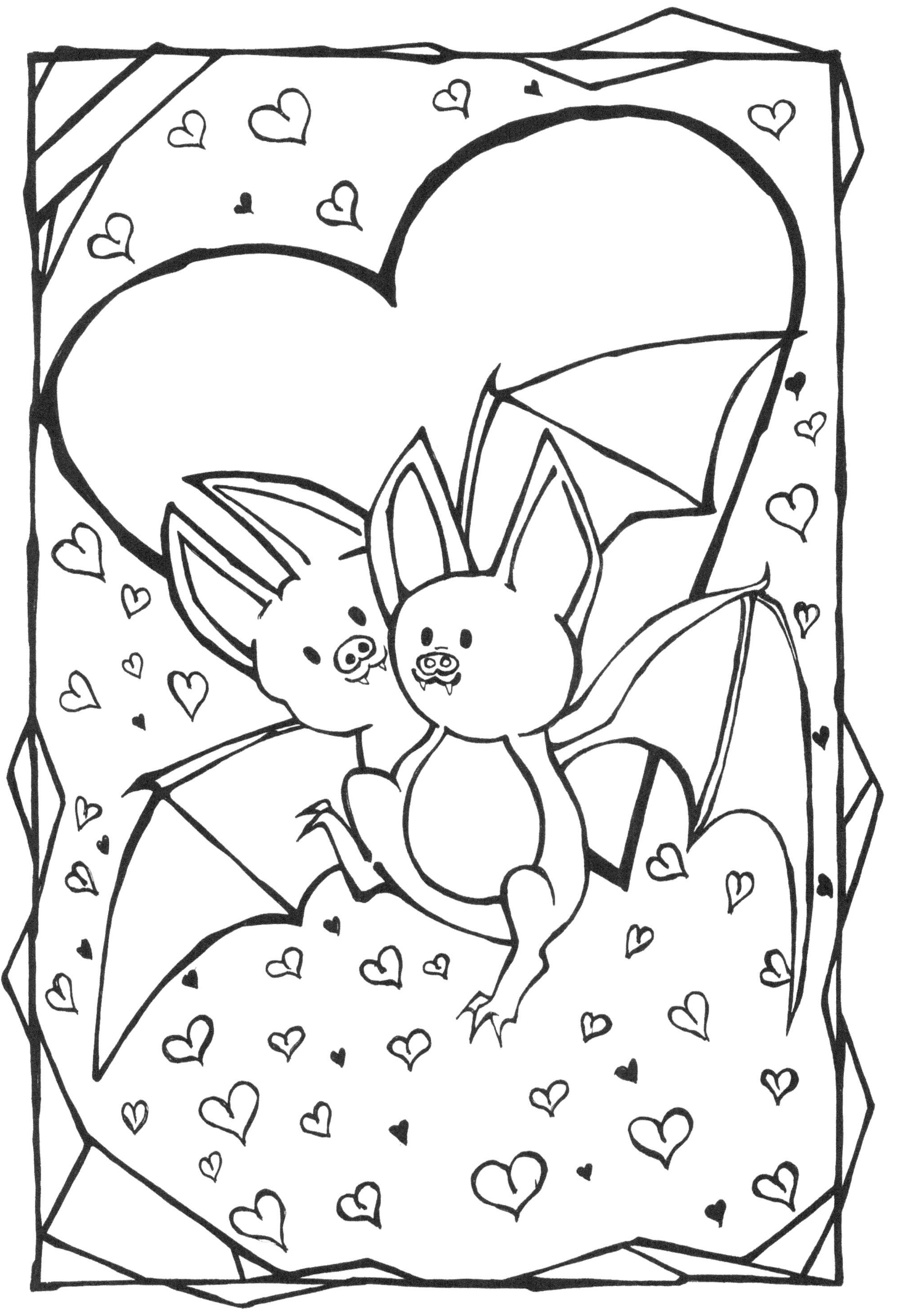

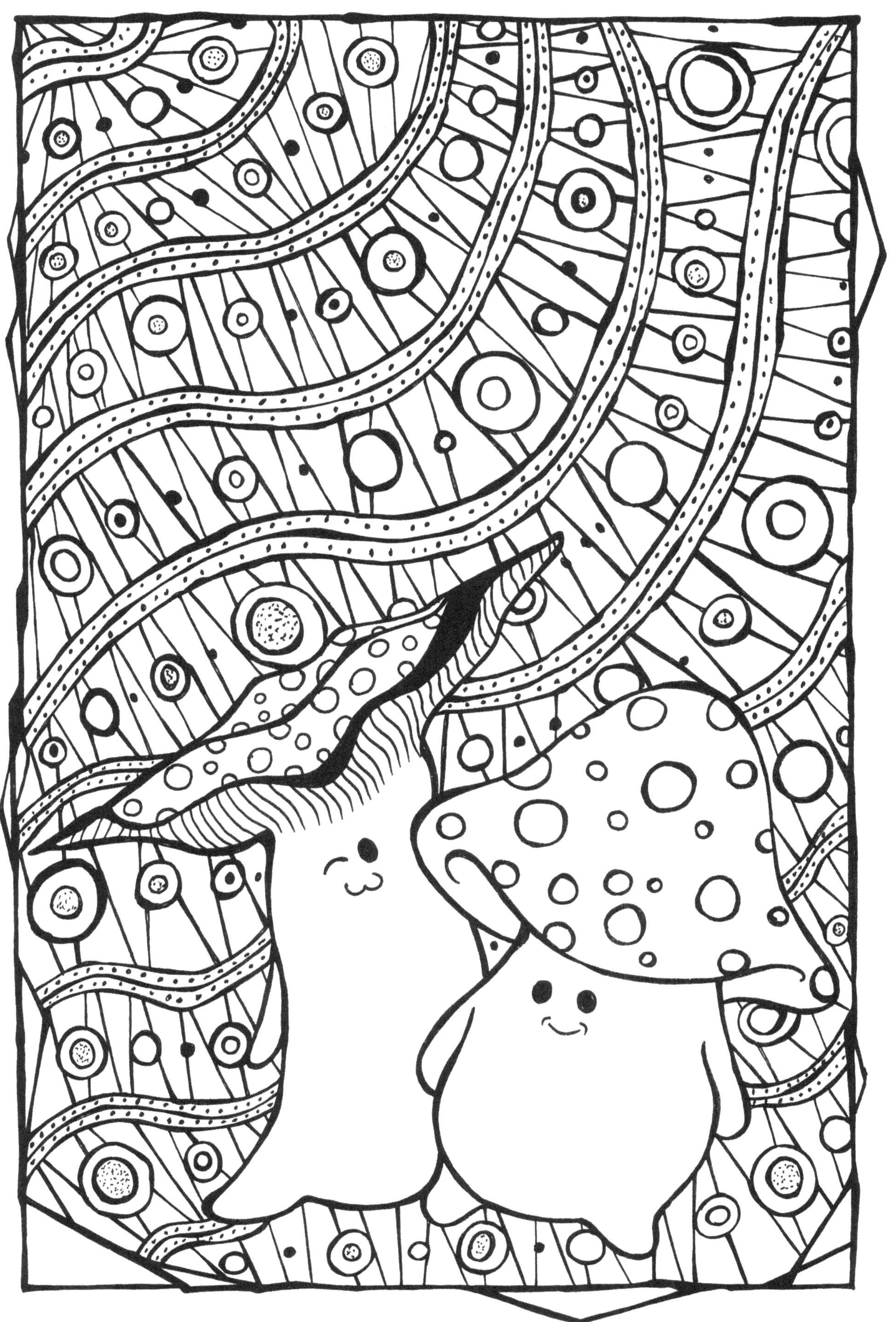

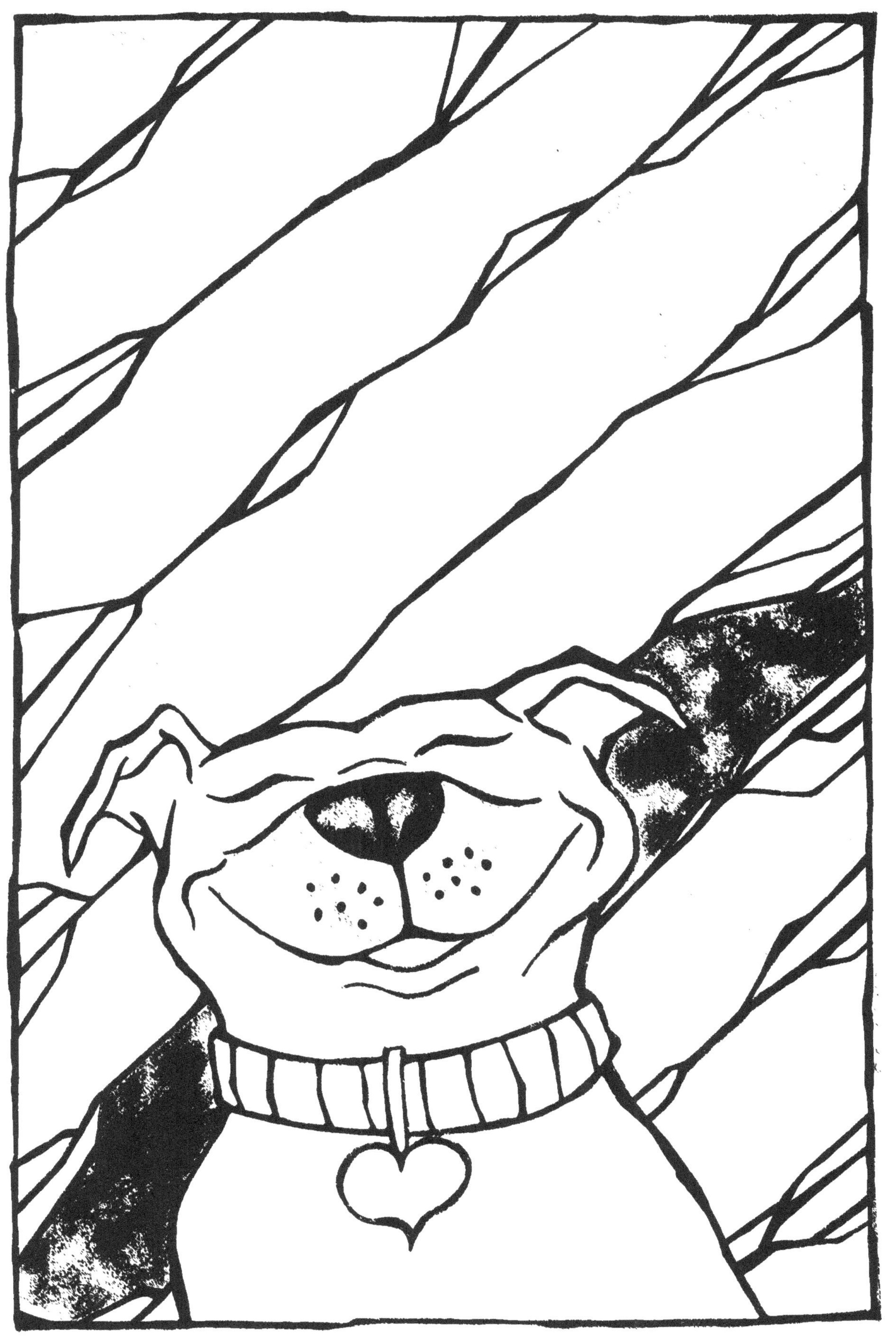

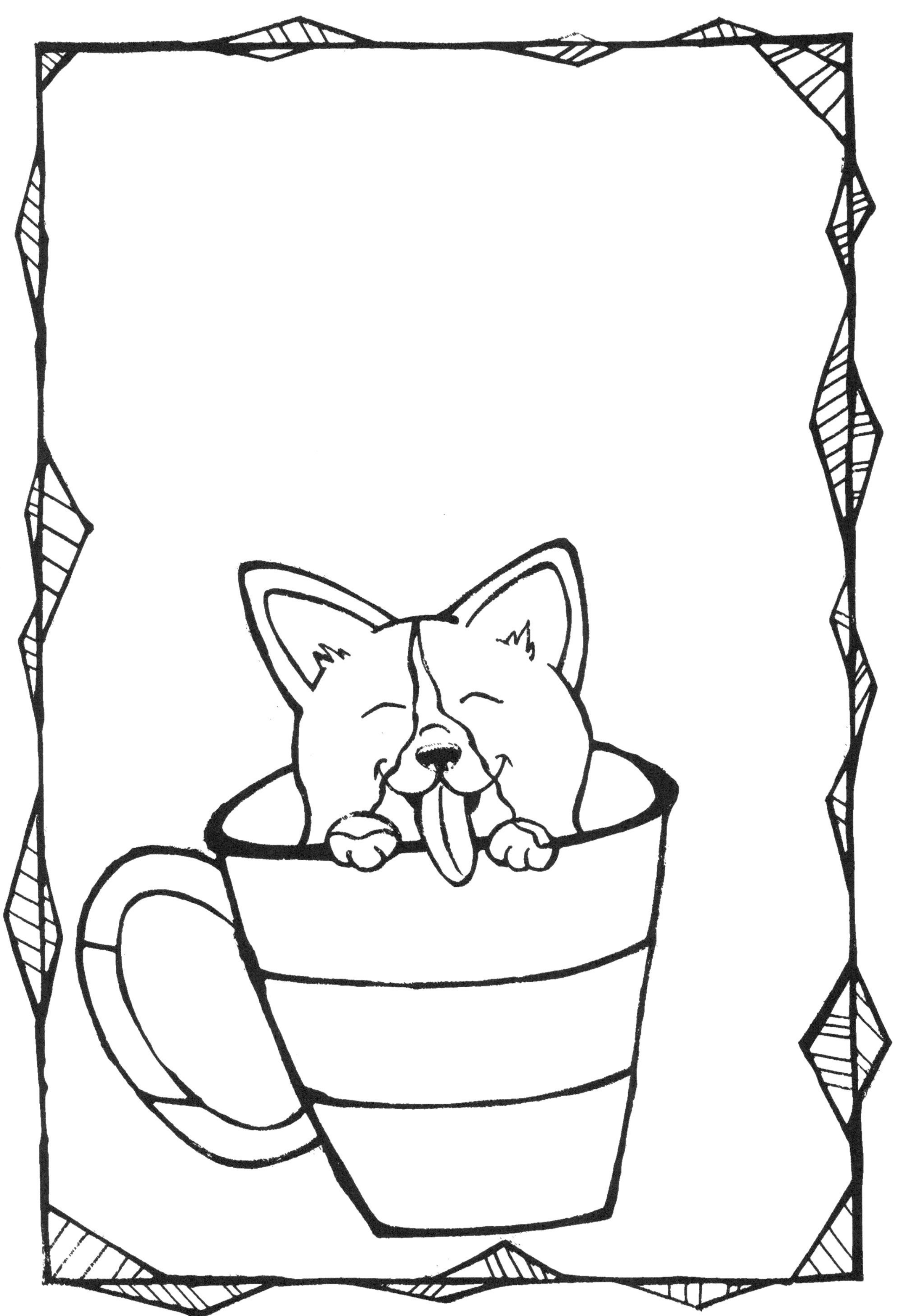

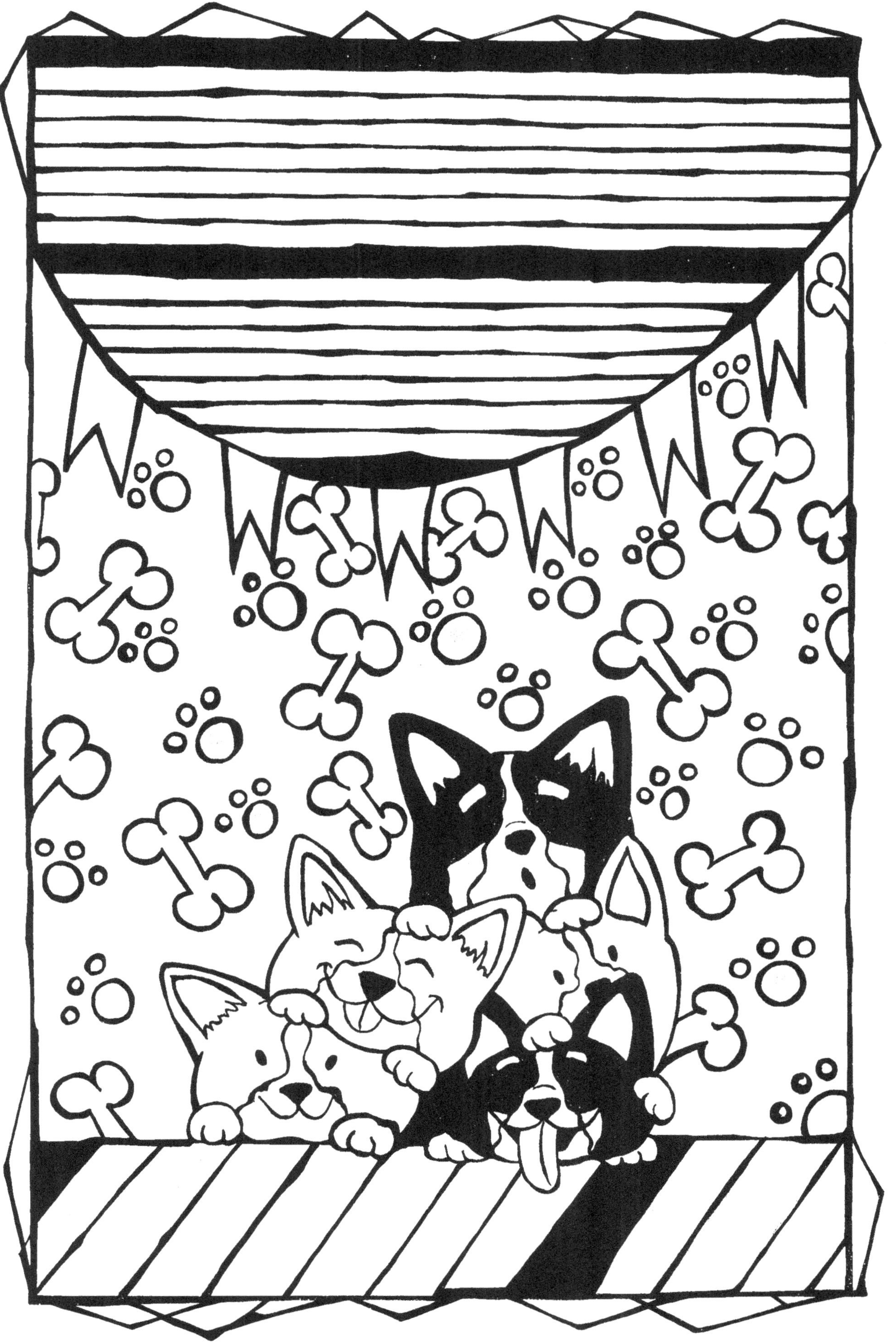

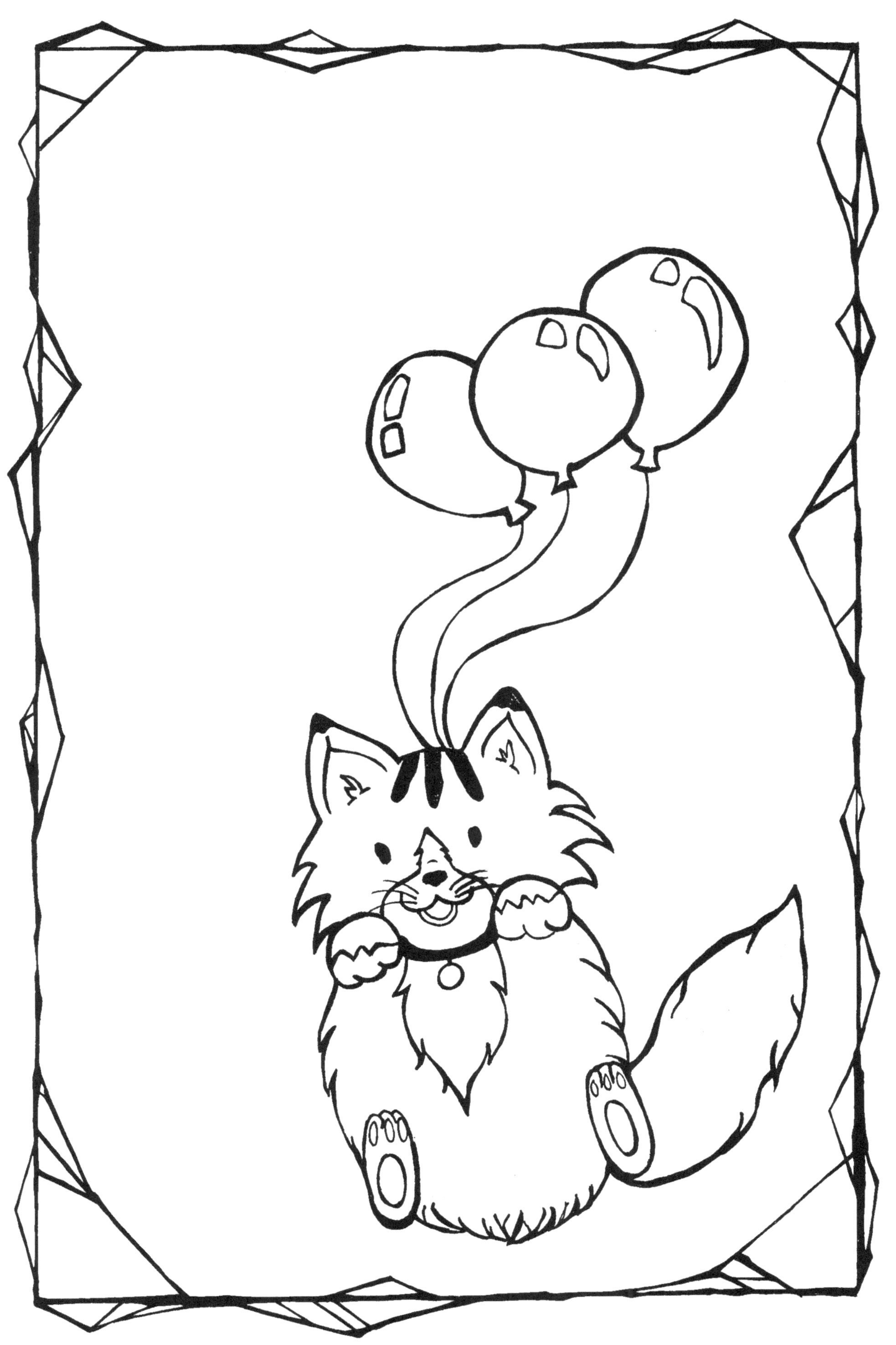